How to Make
Log Cabin Flannel Quilts
with Foundation Piecing
by Linda Causee

Editorial: Bobbie Matela, Linda Causee, Christina Wilson
Graphic Artist: April McArthur, Jessi Butler

Thank you to the following companies who generously supplied products for our blocks:

Bernina® of America: Artista 180 sewing machine

Güterman: 100% cotton sewing thread

Stearns Technical Textile Company: Mountain Mist® White Rose and Cream Rose 100% Cotton Needled Batting

Pictured quilts were made by: Kathryn Causee, Linda Causee, Sandy Hunter, Claire Jungerson, Robin Radovich, Sue Ragan, Michiko Rice, Linda Steiner, and Christina Wilson.

Quilts were quilted by Faith Horsky.

1455 Linda Vista Drive
San Marcos, CA 92069
www.ASNpub.com
©2003 American School of Needlework Inc.

The full line of ASN products is carried by Annie's Attic catalog.
TOLL FREE ORDER LINE or to request a free catalog (800) 582-6643
visit www.AnniesAttic.com
Customer Service (800) 282-6643, Fax (800) 882-6643

We have made every effort to ensure the accuracy and completeness of these instructions. We cannot, however, be responsible for human error, typographical mistakes, or variations in individual work. Reprinting or duplicating the information, photographs or graphics in this publication by any means, including copy machine, computer scanning, digital photography, e-mail, personal Web site and fax, is illegal. Failure to abide by federal copyright laws may result in litigation and fines.

ISBN: 1-59012-071-X   All rights reserved.   Printed in U. S. A.   1 2 3 4 5 6 7 8 9

Introduction

Until recently, flannel fabric was found almost exclusively in the juvenile section of most fabric stores and not at all in quilt shops. Now, many quilt shops have entire sections devoted to flannel fabric. You can find flannel fabric in pastels as well as brights, country as well as modern, florals, geometrics, in fact, something for everyone!

Flannel and quilts seem like the perfect combination—both represent something soft and cozy. But that is not always the case when making a quilt with flannel. Flannel has some unique qualities that sometimes make it a little more challenging to work with. But knowing this, taking a few precautions and using foundation piecing for the simple Log Cabin block will make sewing these blocks fun and easy.

So, pick your favorite Log Cabin flannel quilt, gather your flannel fabrics, make your foundations and create a quilt to cuddle with or use as a wall hanging. Full-size block patterns and directions are given for each quilt as shown, plus layout, yardages and cutting requirements for up to five other sizes.

General Directions

Working with Flannel:
An Overview

Look for flannel that is good quality 100% cotton. There is such a wide variety of colors and prints available that you will be able to make a quilt to suit anyone's taste. The easiest way to choose fabrics for a quilt is to select a colorful "theme" fabric. Once you find one that you absolutely love, choose fabrics that complement and contrast with the theme fabric. For example, the bright floral print in the border of the Springtime Floral quilt, page 56, was selected first, then the fabrics for the flowers were chosen using the colors in the floral print as a guide.

When buying flannel fabrics, keep in mind that they shrink and fray more than regular quilter's cotton fabric. So, to allow for pre-shrinking your fabric, it is recommended that you buy at least yard more of each fabric. **Note:** *The yardage requirements listed with each quilt give the yardage needed; they don't include the extra ¼ yard. Also, check the width of each of your fabrics; flannel fabrics sometimes vary a great deal in width. The fabric amounts given are based on fabric being 40"-wide, so if you have a fabric that is less than 40" wide (remember not to include selvages in your measurement), you may need to buy a little extra.*

Pre-wash flannel in very hot water on the gentlest cycle, then dry on the hottest setting in your dryer. You may want to repeat this process again just to be sure that fabrics are completely pre-shrunk. After washing and drying, you will notice that flannel tends to fray much more than regular cotton fabric. Cut off frayed edges and spray with magic sizing. The sizing will help the fabrics hold their shape when cutting. Press fabrics on wrong side with a dry iron.

Working with shapes that are on straight grain lines (crosswise and lengthwise) is usually recommended for flannel fabrics since they tend to be stretchier than normal cotton fabrics. Therefore, regular piecing with flannel fabrics is generally limited to sewing squares, strips and rectangles.

One advantage to sewing the blocks in this book is that they are foundation pieced. The pieces start out as strips, squares or triangles (cut from squares), but they can end up as irregular shapes such as the odd-shaped triangles in the Flower Blocks, pages 61 to 64; the shapes are formed after sewing and trimming.

Another advantage of foundation piecing is that the blocks are stabilized by the foundation. As long as the blocks remain on the foundation, they will not stretch out of shape. Therefore, it is important that you keep the foundation on the block until after the quilt blocks are sewn together.

Foundation piecing with flannel is easy since the nap of the fabric causes the pieces to "stick" together without pinning. This means that they will not slip out of place as sometimes happens when turning a foundation over to begin piecing.

When piecing with flannel, it is recommended to use a ⅜" to ½" seam allowance. Because of a good deal of fraying that happens with flannel fabric, a larger seam allowance will allow the quilt to wear better and not fall apart with use.

Flannel fabric is much thicker than regular cotton fabric. Therefore, a lot of bulk can be created when seam allowances overlap. Go over these areas slowly when piecing and they should not be a problem. An even-feed foot is a great help when going over thick areas.

Flannel fabric will dull a needle quicker; therefore, you will have to change your needle more often.

Flannel will also create more lint in your sewing machine. Be sure to clean the bobbin case and under the throat plate regularly. Check it every time you change a bobbin to be on the safe side.

About the Blocks

The Log Cabin blocks in these quilts range from the very traditional to the very modern. They measure 5" and 7" square.

Foundation Piecing

The easiest and most accurate way to piece Log Cabin blocks is the foundation method. It eliminates the need to cut out each piece exactly.

Your first consideration is what type of foundation to use for piecing your blocks. There are several options. A light-colored, lightweight cotton fabric or muslin are popular choices. A lightweight fabric needs to be light enough to see through to trace onto. Of course, it will add another layer of fabric that you will have to quilt through, but it will give extra stability to your blocks. Another choice for foundations is paper. Use any paper that you can see through for easy tracing—notebook paper, copy paper, newsprint, or computer papers are a few options. Then, tear paper away after sewing is completed. A third choice is Tear Away® interfacing. Like, muslin, it is light enough to see through for tracing, but like paper, it can later be easily removed before quilting.

A new type of "disappearing" foundation material by W. H. Collins is called Wash-Away™ foundation paper. After sewing, place block in water and the foundation dissolves in 10 seconds.

Mirror Images

Log Cabin blocks, in general, are not symmetrical, therefore a mirror image of the block pattern will be produced when pieced, **Fig 1**. On each pattern page, there is a small diagram showing how the block will look once it has been pieced. Note whether it is a mirror image of the block pattern and consider that when choosing fabric and planning your quilt layout.

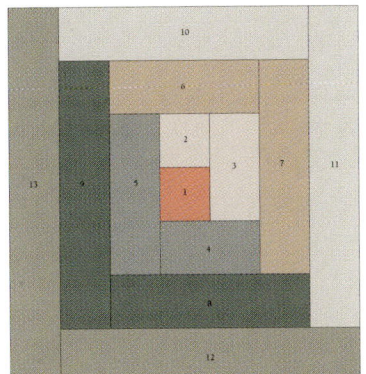

Pattern

Finished Block

Fig 1

Preparing the Foundation
Tracing the Block

Trace the block pattern carefully onto your chosen foundation material. Use a ruler and a fine-point permanent marker to make straight lines and be sure to include all numbers. Draw a line ¼" from outside edges of block, **Fig 2**; cut along this outside drawn line. Repeat for the needed number of blocks for your quilt.

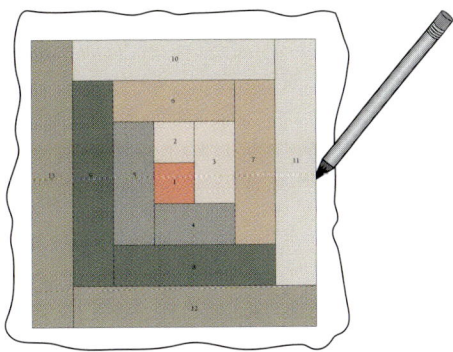

Fig 2

Hint: If you want your finished block to have the same direction as the block pattern, you must first trace onto tracing paper, then flop pattern and trace onto foundation material, Fig 3.

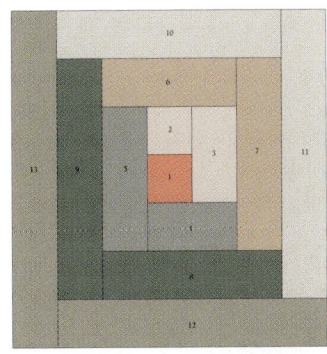

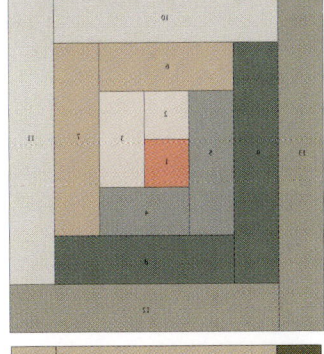

Fig 3

Transferring the Block

The block pattern can also be transferred onto foundation material using a transfer pen or pencil. Trace the block pattern onto paper using a transfer pen or pencil. Then following manufacturer's directions, iron transfer onto foundation material. Write numbers on foundation using a fine-point permanent marking pen. The block, when pieced, will look like the pattern as it appears in the book, but will be a mirror image to the completed block shown in the color photographs.

Hint: If you want your Log Cabin block to look like the completed block shown in color and you are using a transfer pen or pencil (for example, you want the Log Cabin block to spin clockwise), transfer as described above. But, if you would like your Log Cabin block to spin counterclockwise, you must trace first with a permanent pen onto tracing paper, flop the traced design and trace again with the transfer pen or pencil.

Cutting the Fabric

The beauty of foundation piecing is that you do not have to cut every exact piece for every block. When using flannel fabric, it is best to start out with pieces that are on the straight grain of the fabric—you can use strips, rectangles, squares or triangles cut from squares. You do have to be careful to use a piece of fabric that is at least ⅜" to ½" larger on all sides than the space it is to cover. Triangle shapes can be a little tricky to piece. Use generous-sized fabric pieces and be careful when positioning the pieces onto the foundation. You do waste some fabric this way, but the time it saves in cutting will be worth it in the end.

Hint: Cut strips the width needed for the spaces on the block. If the space is 1" wide, add ½" seam allowance on each side and cut 2"-wide strips. If desired, cut strips the exact lengths needed for each "log." For example, if the log is 3" long, cut strip 4" long (includes ½" seam allowance at each end). Once strips are all cut, stack strips in numerical order to make piecing easier and quicker.

How to Make a Foundation-Pieced Block

Prepare foundations as described in Preparing the Foundation, page 5.

1. Turn foundation with unmarked side facing you and position piece 1 over the space marked 1 on the foundation. Hold foundation up to a light source to make sure that fabric overlaps at least ¼" on all sides of space 1, **Fig 4**; pin or glue in place with a glue stick.

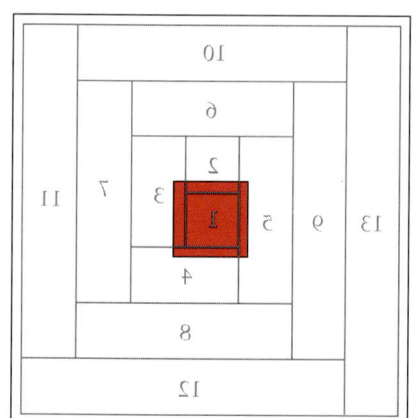

Fig 4

2. Place fabric piece 2 right sides together with piece 1. *Note: Double check to see if fabric piece chosen will cover space 2 completely by folding over along line between space 1 and 2, **Fig 5**.*

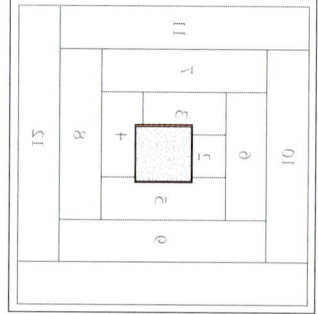

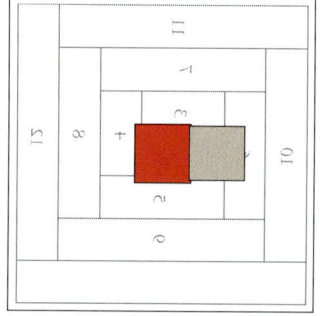

Fig 5

3. Turn foundation with marked side facing you and fold foundation forward along line between spaces 1 and 2; trim both pieces about ¼" above fold line, **Fig 6**.

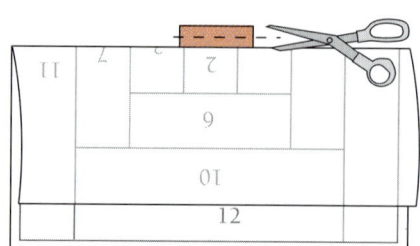

Fig 6

4. With marked side of foundation still facing you, sew along line between spaces 1 and 2 using a very small stitch (to allow for easier paper removal), **Fig 7**; begin and end two to three stitches beyond line.

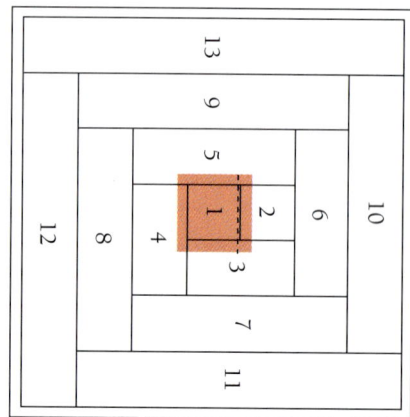

Fig 7

5. Turn foundation over. Open piece 2 and finger press along seam, **Fig 8**. Use a pin or a dab of glue stick to hold piece in place.

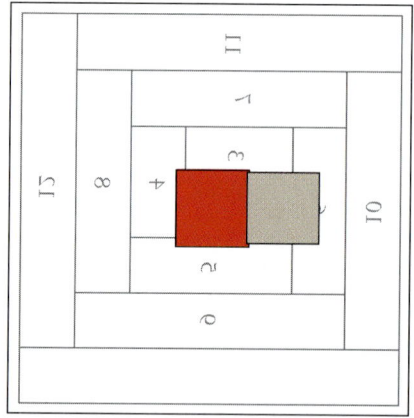

Fig 8

6. Turn foundation with marked side facing you; fold foundation forward along line between spaces 2 and 3 and trim piece 2 about ¼" from fold, **Fig 9**.

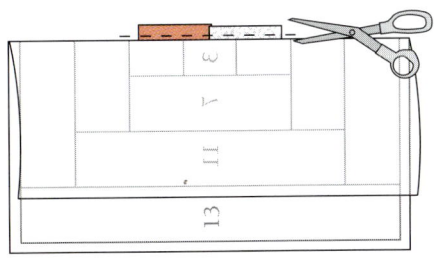

Fig 9

7. Place fabric 3 right side down even with just-trimmed edge, **Fig 10**.

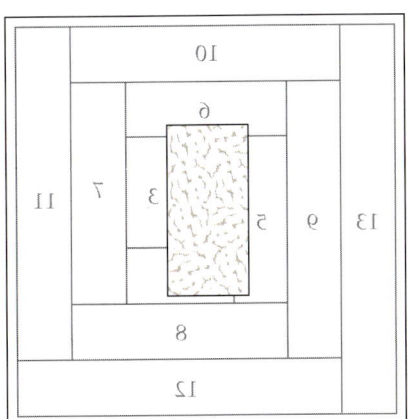

Fig 10

8. Turn foundation to marked side and sew along line between spaces 2 and 3; begin and end sewing 2 or 3 stitches beyond line, **Fig 11**.

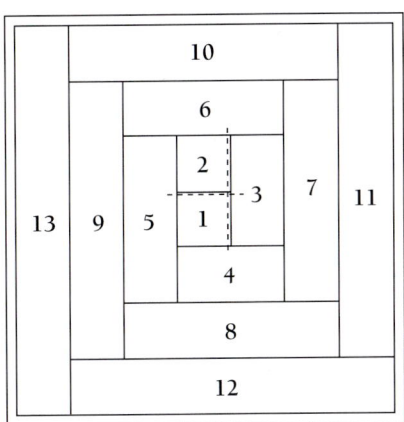

Fig 11

9. Turn foundation over, open piece 3 and finger press seam, **Fig 12**. Glue or pin in place.

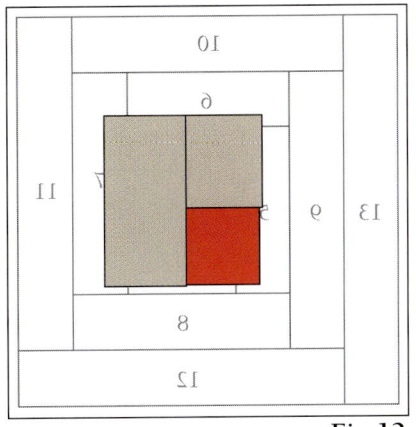

Fig 12

10. Turn foundation with marked side facing you; fold foundation forward along line between spaces 1, 2 and 4. If previous stitching makes it difficult to fold foundation forward, pull paper foundation away from fabric at stitching, then fold along line. If using a fabric foundation, fold it forward as far as it will go and trim to about ¼" from drawn line, **Fig 13**.

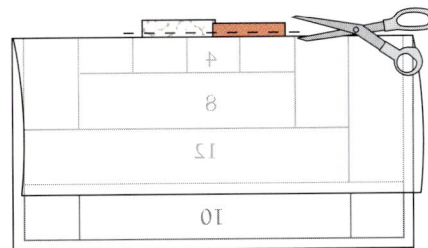

Fig 13

11. Sew along line between spaces 1, 3 and 4, **Fig 14**.

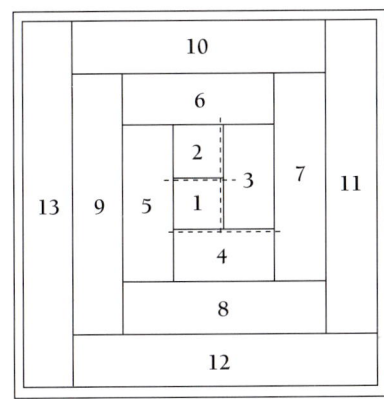

Fig 14

12. Continue trimming and sewing pieces in numerical order until block is complete. Make sure pieces along outer edge are large enough to allow for a ½" seam allowance. Press block, then trim fabric even with outside line of foundation, **Fig 15**, to complete block, **Fig 16**.

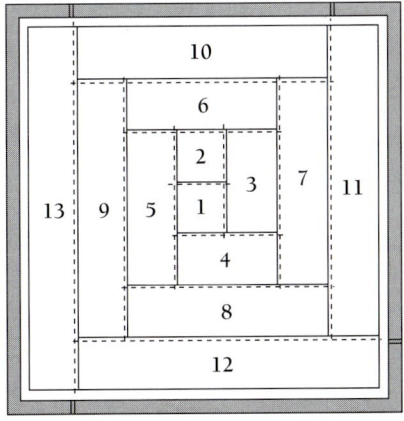

Fig 15

Fig 16

*Hint: Do not remove paper yet. It is better to remove paper after blocks have been sewn together since flannel tends to stretch and may become distorted. Staystitching along outer edge of block, **Fig 17**, will also help keep fabric from stretching out of shape.*

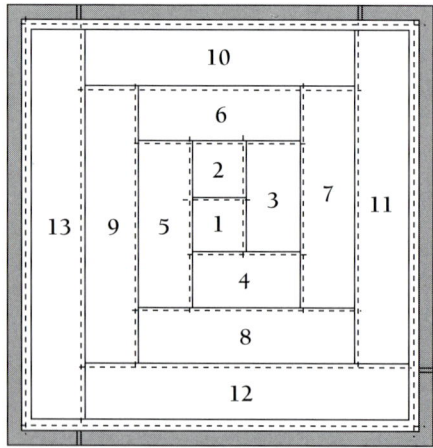

Fig 17

Highlights and Hints for Foundation Piecing with Flannel

- Put a dab of glue stick or pin first piece to foundation.
- Begin and end sewing at least two to three stitches beyond line on which you are sewing, **Fig 18**.

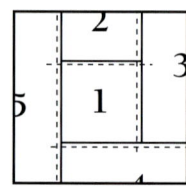

Fig 18

- Be careful not to stretch fabric as you sew. Just lay fabric pieces on top of each other. The fuzziness of the fabric will hold them together for sewing.
- Finger press after every seam. The little wooden "irons" found in quilt shops or catalogs work great.
- Use a short stitch, around 18 to 20 stitches per inch.

- Trim seam allowances ⅜" to ½" when working with flannel.
- Don't worry too much about the stretchiness of the flannel. Sewing to a foundation stabilizes the fabric and will prevent it from getting out of shape.
- When sewing spaces with points, it is easier to start sewing from the wide end towards the point, **Fig 19**.

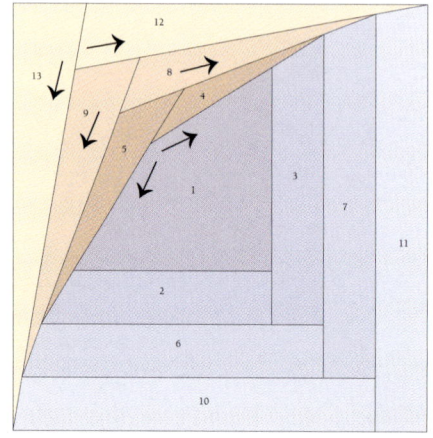

Fig 19

- Directional prints are not recommended unless they are used only once in a block or placed where they can be used easily in a consistent manner, **Fig 20**.

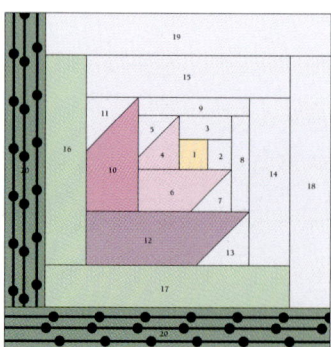
Like this

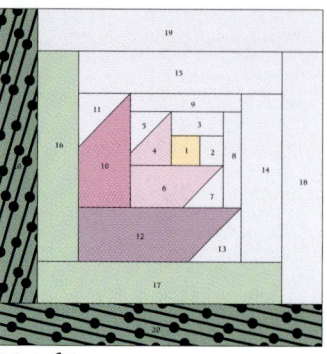
Not this

Fig 20

Making a Quilt Top

Sew blocks (and sashing) in rows; sew rows together.

Measure quilt top lengthwise; cut two border strips to that length and sew to sides of quilt. Measure quilt top crosswise, including borders just added and cut two border strips to that length. Sew to top and bottom of quilt top. Repeat for any remaining borders.

The cutting instructions with the patterns suggest cutting strips along the crosswise grain. When border strips longer than the width of the fabric are needed, you will need to piece two or more strips together to achieve the necessary length. Place strips perpendicular to each other with right sides together, **Fig 21**. Stitch diagonally starting from outside corner, **Fig 22**. Trim fabric ½" from stitching, **Fig 23** and press seam open.

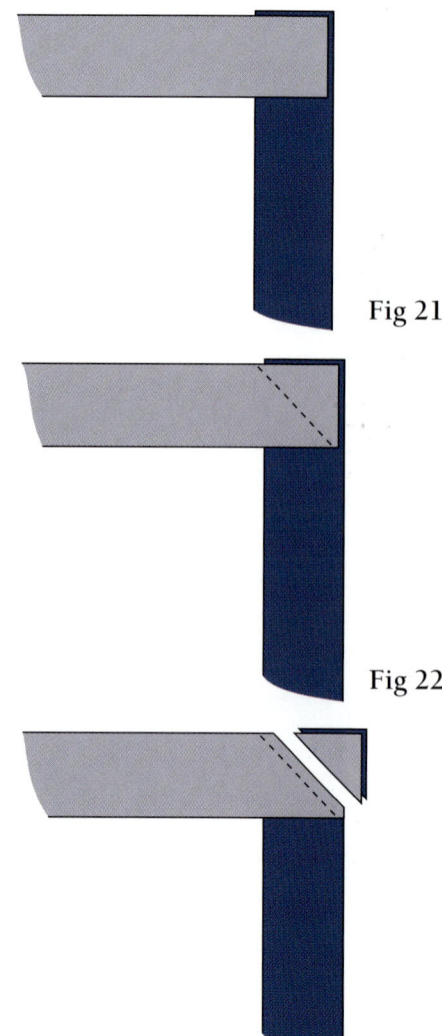

Fig 21

Fig 22

Fig 23

If used, remove paper or Tear Away® backing at this time. **Hint:** *Use a spray bottle of water to dampen paper for easier removal.*

Finishing Your Quilt
Marking the Quilting Design

Before marking on your quilt top, be sure to test any marking material to make sure it will wash out of your fabric. Mark all quilting lines on the right side of the fabric. For marking, use a hard lead pencil, chalk or other special quilt marking materials. If you quilt right on the marked lines, they will not show.

A word of caution: Marking lines which are intended to disappear after quilting—either by exposure to air or with water—may become permanent when set with a hot iron. Therefore, don't iron your quilt top after you have marked your quilting pattern.

If you are quilting around shapes, you may not need to mark the lines if you feel that you can accurately gauge the quilting line as you work. If you are quilting "in the ditch" of the seam (the space right in the seam), marking is not necessary. Other quilting will need to be marked.

If you plan to tie your quilt, you do not need to mark it.

Attaching the Batting and Backing

There are a number of different types of batting on the market. There are several different types of batting on the market. The type you choose is personal preference.

Hint: Remove batting from its packaging a day in advance and open it out full size. This will help the batting to lie flat.

Use 100% cotton flannel fabric for the backing of your quilt. If you are making a quilt wider than the 42"-wide fabrics, you will have to piece your fabric to fit the quilt top. Cut off the selvages and sew pieces together carefully; press seams open. Cut batting and backing about 2" larger than the quilt top on all sides. Place backing, wrong side up, on a flat surface. Place batting centered on top of backing, then center quilt right side up on batting.

The layers of the quilt must now be held together before quilting. Baste layers together using one of the following techniques:

Fusible iron-on batting – The new Fusible Batting™ by June Tailor and Gold-Fuse by Mountain Mist® are wonderful new ways to hold the quilt layers together without using other time-consuming methods of basting.

Thread basting - Baste with long stitches, starting in the center and sewing toward the edges in a number of diagonal lines. Use more basting stitches when working with flannel fabric.

Safety pin basting - Pin through all layers at once starting from the center and working out to the edges. Place the pins no more than 4" apart. Think of your quilt plan as you work and make certain that your pins avoid the prospective quilting lines. Choose rustproof pins that are #1 or #2. To make pinning easier, many quilters use a quilter's spoon. The spoon is notched so that it can push the point of the safety pins closed.

Quilt gun basting - Use the handy trigger tool (found in quilt and fabric stores) that pushes nylon tags through all layers of the quilt. Start in the center and work randomly toward the outside edges. Place tags about 4" apart. You can sew right over the tags and then they can be easily removed by cutting off with a pair of scissors.

Spray or heat set basting – Use one of the spray adhesives currently on the market, following manufacturer's directions.

Quilting

Your quilt can be either machine or hand quilted or tied. The extra thickness of flannel makes hand quilting in the traditional sense more difficult.

If you would like to hand quilt, use a thicker thread such as #5 pearl cotton, a large needle and use a long running stitch, **Fig 24**. This gives the quilt a homey look which is a great complement for a flannel quilt.

Fig 24

Note: Hand quilting will also be more difficult if fabric or muslin was used as a foundation since there is an extra layer of fabric to quilt through.

If you have never used a sewing machine for quilting, you might want to read more about the technique. Learn to Machine Quilt in Just One Weekend (ASN #4186), by Marti Michell is an excellent introduction to machine quilting. This book is available at your local quilt store or department, or write the publisher for a list of sources.

You do not need a special machine for quilting. You can machine quilt with almost any home sewing machine. Just make sure that it is oiled and in good working condition. An even-feed foot is a good investment if you are going to machine quilt since it is designed to feed the top and bottom layers of the quilt through the machine evenly.

Use fine transparent nylon thread in the top and regular sewing thread in the bobbin.

To quilt in the ditch of a seam (this is actually stitching in the space between two pieces of fabric that have been sewn together), use your fingers to pull the blocks or pieces apart and machine stitch right between the two pieces. Try to keep your stitching just to the side of the seam that does not have the bulk of the seam allowance under it. When you have finished stitching, the quilting will be practically hidden in the seam.

Free form machine quilting is done with a darning foot and the feed dogs down on your sewing machine. It can be used to quilt around a design or to quilt a motif. Mark your quilting design as described in Marking the Quilting Design on page 9. Free form machine quilting takes practice to master because you are controlling the quilt through the machine rather than the machine moving the quilt. With free form machine quilting, you can quilt in any direction—up and down, side-to-side and even in circles without pivoting the quilt around the needle.

If you would like to tie your quilt, thread a length of six strands of embroidery floss, #5 or #8 pearl cotton or yarn in a large tapestry needle. Curved quilter's needles also work very well. Following **Fig 25**, push needle through quilt from top to back (A), leaving a short tail; bring needle up a short distance away (B). Go back down (A) and up (B) through original holes.

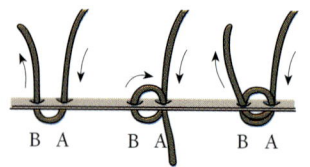

Fig 25

Tie ends into a double bow, **Fig 26**, and trim to 1". Repeat knots at corners and random areas of blocks.

Fig 26

Note: If you do not want loose ends on the front of your quilt, repeat above steps except start from the back and tie knot on back of quilt.

Attaching the Binding

For flannel quilts, a single-fold binding is recommended. Trim backing and batting even with quilt top. Cut enough 2"-wide strips to go around all four sides of quilt, plus 6". Join strips end-to-end with diagonal seams; trim corners, **Fig 27**.

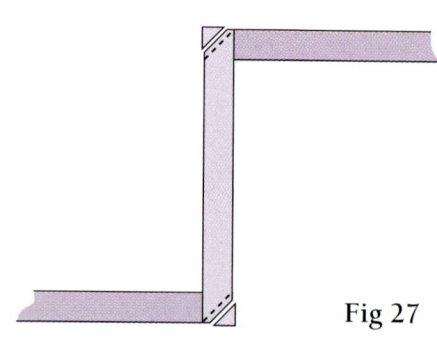

Fig 27

Press seams open. Cut one end of strip at a 45-degree angle, then press under ¼", **Fig 28**.

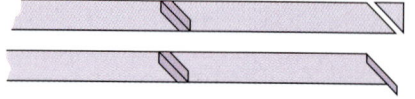

Fig 28

Press under ¼" along one lengthwise edge of strip, **Fig 29**.

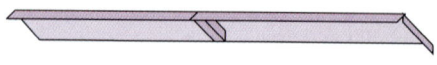

Fig 29

On right side of quilt, position binding in middle of one side, aligning raw edges. Sew binding to quilt using ½" seam allowance, beginning about an inch below folded end of binding, **Fig 30**.

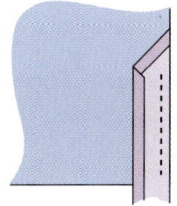

Fig 30

At corner, stop ¼" from edge of quilt and backstitch. Fold binding away from quilt at a 45-degree angle. Fold binding back on itself so fold is on quilt edge and raw edges are aligned with adjacent side of quilt, **Fig 31**. Begin sewing at quilt edge.

Fig 31

Continue in same manner around remaining sides of quilt. To finish, stop about two inches away from starting point. Trim excess binding, then tuck inside folded end, **Fig 32**. Finish line of stitching.

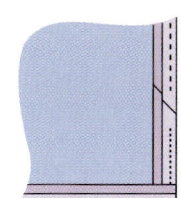

Fig 32

Fold binding to back of quilt so seamline is covered; blindstitch in place.

The Finishing Touch

When your quilt is finished, always sign and date it. A label can be cross-stitched, embroidered or even written with a permanent marking pen. Hand stitch to back of quilt.

Attic Windows

Approximate Size: 44" x 49"
Small Lap Size Setting: 6 x 7
Number of Blocks: 42

Materials

Note: The fabric amounts given are based on what is needed for this project. Due to flannel shrinkage, you may want to purchase at least ¼ to ½ yd more of each fabric.

½ to 1 yd novelty print
⅜ yd lt blue
⅜ yd dk blue
⅜ yd lt burgundy
½ yd dk burgundy
⅜ yd gold print fabric (first border)
1 yd novelty print (allow more if print is directional)
⅜ yd dk blue (binding)
2 yds backing
Twin-size batting

Cutting Requirements

Note: All strips include ½" seam allowance.
Cut the following 2"-wide strips for piecing:
Five strips, lt blue
Six strips, dk blue
Six strips, lt burgundy
Seven strips, dk burgundy

Cut the following for "window":
42 – 4" squares, novelty (The squares in the photographed model were fussy-cut.)

Cut the following border and binding strips:
Four 3"-wide strips, gold print (first border)
Five 6"-wide strips, novelty print (second border)
Five 2"-wide strips, dk blue (binding)

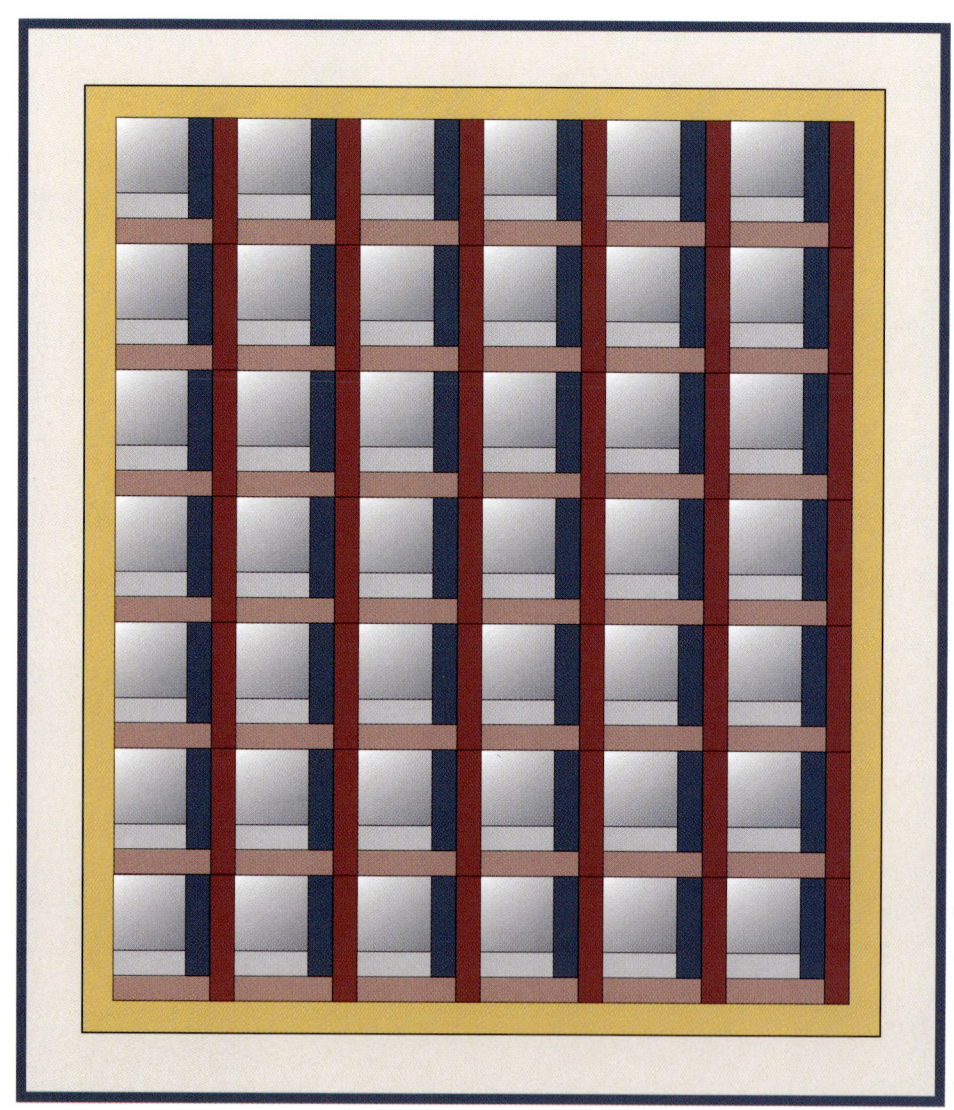

Quilt Diagram

Instructions

Note: Read Working with Flannel: An Overview, page 4 before beginning. Use ½" seam allowance for sewing.

1. Refer to How to Make a Foundation-pieced block, pages 6 to 8, and make 42 Log Cabin blocks using pattern on page 17.

Continued on page 14

2. Arrange blocks in seven rows of six blocks according to photograph (or your own desired layout).
3. Sew blocks together in rows; then sew rows together. Press seams in alternate directions.
4. Measure quilt top lengthwise; piece 3"-wide border strips (if necessary) to achieve needed length (refer to Making a Quilt Top, pages 8 to 11, for piecing border strips); repeat for another strip. Sew strips to opposite sides of quilt top. Press seams toward border.
5. Measure quilt top crosswise, including borders just added; piece 3"-wide border strips (if necessary) to achieve needed length; repeat for another strip. Sew strips to top and bottom of quilt top. Press seams toward border.
6. Repeat steps 4 and 5 for 6"-wide borders.
7. Finish quilt referring to Finishing Your Quilt, pages 9 to 11.

Other Sizes

The following chart shows number of strips or squares needed to make the number of Log Cabin blocks for five other quilt sizes. Block and strips are cut 2" for the Wall hanging/Baby size and 2½" wide for remaining sizes.

	Wall hanging/Baby	Twin	Full	Queen	King
Size	37" x 37"	70" x 91"	83" x 97"	93" x 100"	104" x 104"
Setting	5 x 5	8 x 11	9 x 11	10 x 11	12 x 12
Blocks	25	88	99	110	144
Novelty print center squares	25 @ 4"	88 @ 4"	99 @ 4"	110 @ 4"	144 @ 4"
Lt blue	3	11	13	14	18
Dk blue	4	15	17	19	24
Lt burgundy	4	15	17	19	24
Dk burgundy	5	18	20	22	29
Border 1	4 @ 3" wide	7 @ 3" wide	7 @ 3" wide	8 @ 3" wide	9 @ 3" wide
Border 2	4 @ 5" wide	9 @ 6" wide	8 @ 4" wide	9 @ 4½" wide	10 @ 4" wide
Border 3	-	-	9 @ 6" wide	10 @ 7" wide	11 @5" wide
Binding	4 @ 2" wide	9 @ 2" wide	9 @ 2" wide	10 @ 2" wide	11 @ 2" wide

Note: *The border widths are the cut measurements.*

The following chart shows the yardage needed for each size quilt.

Yardage					
Novelty print (centers)	½-1 yd	2-2½ yds	2-2½ yds	2½-3 yds	3-3½ yds
Lt blue	¼ yd	1 yd	1⅛ yds	1¼ yds	1⅝ yds
Dk blue	¼ yd	1¼ yds	1½ yds	1⅝ yds	2⅛ yds
Lt burgundy	¼ yd	1¼ yds	1½ yds	1⅝ yds	2⅛ yds
Dk burgundy	⅜ yd	1½ yds	1¾ yds	2 yds	2½ yds
Border 1	½ yd	⅝ yd	⅝ yd	¾ yds	⅞ yd
Border 2	⅝ yd	1½ yds	1 yd	1¼ yds	1½ yds
Border 3	-	-	1⅜ yds	2 yds	1⅞ yds
Binding	¼ yd	⅝ yd	⅝ yd	¾ yd	¾ yd
Backing	1⅛ yds	5¼ yds	5½ yds	8 yds	9 yds

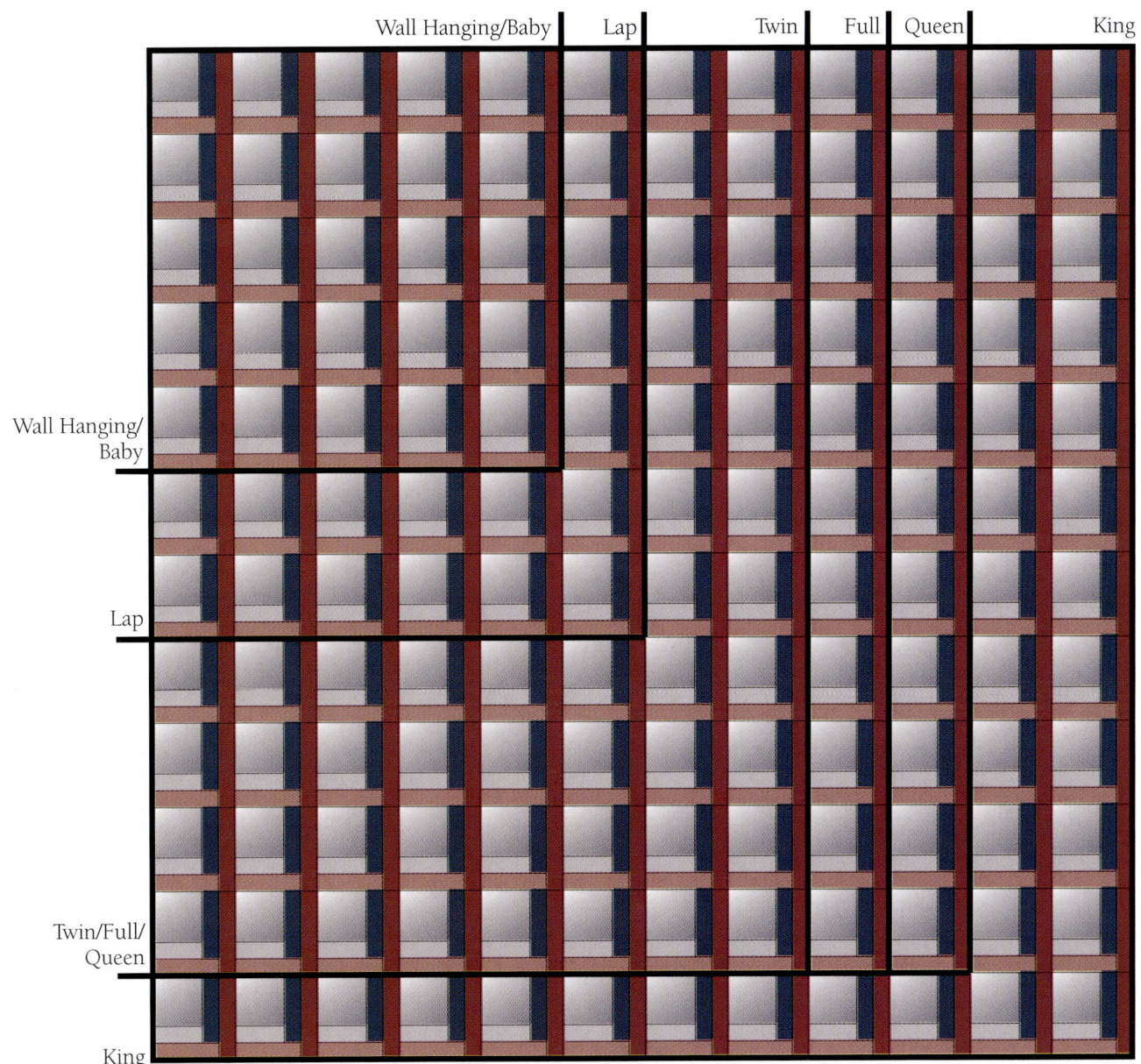

Layout for Other Sizes

15

Attic Windows–7" Block

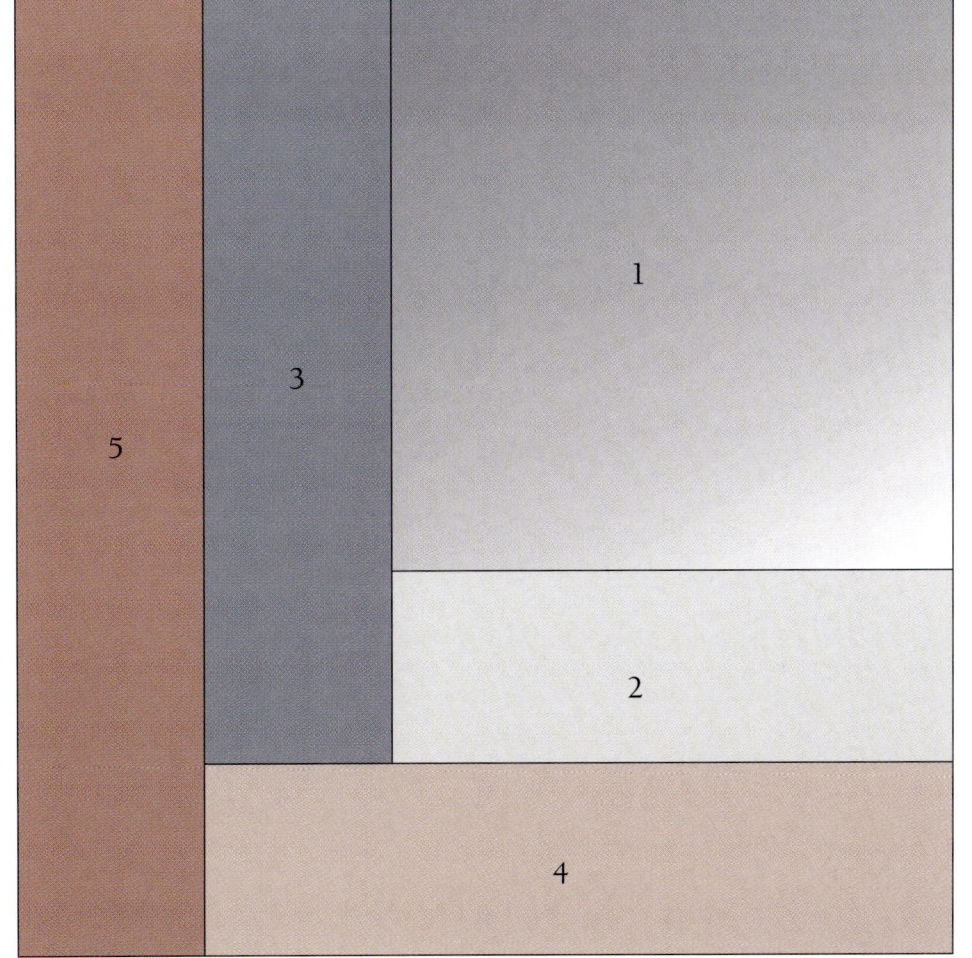

Attic Windows–5" Block

Block Diagram

Rose Garden

Approximate Size: 58" x 72"
Lap Size Setting: 6 x 8
Number of Blocks: 48

Materials

Note: The fabric amounts given are based on what is needed for this project. Due to flannel shrinkage, you may want to purchase at least ¼ to ½ yd more of each fabric.

¼ yd center square fabric
½ yd light fabric 1 (logs 2,3)
¾ yd light fabric 2 (logs 6,7)
1 yd light fabric 3 (logs 10,11)
¾ yd dark fabric 1 (logs 4,5)
1 yd dark fabric 2 (logs 8,9)
1½ yds dark fabric 3 (logs 12, 13)
¾ yd border 1 fabric
1¾ yds border 2 fabric
¾ yd binding fabric
3½ yds backing fabric
Twin-size batting

Cutting Requirements

Note: All strips include ½" seam allowance.

Cut the following 2"-wide strips for piecing:

Three strips, center square fabric
Seven strips, light fabric 1
12 strips, light fabric 2
17 strips, light fabric 3
10 strips, dark fabric 1
15 strips, dark fabric 2
23 strips, dark fabric 3

Cut the following border and binding strips:
Six 3"-wide strips, border 1 fabric
Six 7"-wide strips, border 2 fabric
Seven 2½"-wide strips, binding fabric

Quilt Diagram

Instructions

Note: Read Working with Flannel: An Overview, page 4 before beginning.

1. Refer to How to Make a Foundation-Pieced Block, pages 6 to 8, and make 48 Log Cabin blocks using pattern on page 23.

2. Arrange blocks in eight rows of six blocks according to photograph (or your own desired layout).

3. Sew blocks together in rows, then sew rows together. Press seams in alternate directions.

4. Measure quilt top lengthwise; piece

Continued on page 20

3"-wide border strips to achieve needed length (refer to Making a Quilt Top, page 8, for piecing border strips); repeat for another strip. Sew strips to opposite sides of quilt top. Press seams toward border.

5. Measure quilt top crosswise, including borders just added; piece 3"-wide border strips to achieve needed length; repeat for another strip. Sew strips to top and bottom of quilt top. Press seams toward border.

6. Repeat steps 5 and 6 for 7"-wide border strips.
7. Finish quilt referring to Finishing Your Quilt, pages 9 to 11.

Other Sizes

The following chart shows number of strips needed to make the number of Log Cabin blocks for five other quilt sizes.

	Wall hanging/Baby	Twin	Full	Queen	King
Size	40" x 40"	68" x 89"	78" x 99"	94" x 100"	104" x 104"
Setting	4 x 4	8 x 11	8 x 11	10 x 11	12 x 12
Blocks	16	88	88	110	144
Center Square strips	1	5	5	6	8
Lt fabric 1	3	12	12	14	19
Dk fabric 1	4	16	16	20	26
Lt fabric 2	5	20	20	25	33
Dk fabric 2	6	25	25	31	40
Lt fabric 3	6	29	29	36	47
Dk fabric 3	7	34	34	42	55
Border 1	4 @ 3" wide	7 @ 3" wide	7 @ 3" wide	8 @ 4" wide	9 @ 4" wide
Border 2	4 @ 5" wide	8 @ 5" wide	7 @ 3" wide	8 @ 3" wide	10 @ 8" wide
Border 3	-	-	9 @ 7" wide	9 @ 8" wide	-
Binding	5 @ 3" wide	8 @ 3" wide	9 @ 3" wide	10 @ 3" wide	11 @ 3" wide

Note: The border widths are the cut measurements.

The following chart shows the yardage needed for each size quilt.

Yardage

	Wall hanging/Baby	Twin	Full	Queen	King
Center Square strips	⅛ yd	⅜ yd	⅜ yd	½ yd	½ yd
Lt fabric 1	¼ yd	¾ yd	¾ yd	⅞ yd	1⅛ yds
Dk fabric 1	⅓ yd	1 yd	1 yd	1¼ yds	1½ yds
Lt fabric 2	⅜ yd	1¼ yds	1¼ yds	1½ yds	1⅞ yds
Dk fabric 2	½ yd	1½ yds	1½ yds	1¾ yds	2⅜ yds
Lt fabric 3	½ yd	1¾ yds	1¾ yds	2⅛ yds	2¾ yds
Dk fabric 3	½ yd	2 yds	2 yds	2½ yds	3⅛ yds
Border 1	⅜ yd	⅝ yd	⅝ yd	1 yd	1⅛ yds
Border 2	⅝ yd	1¼ yds	⅝ yd	¾ yd	2⅜ yds
Border 3	-	-	1⅞ yds	2⅛ yds	-
Binding	½ yd	¾ yd	⅞ yd	1 yd	1 yd

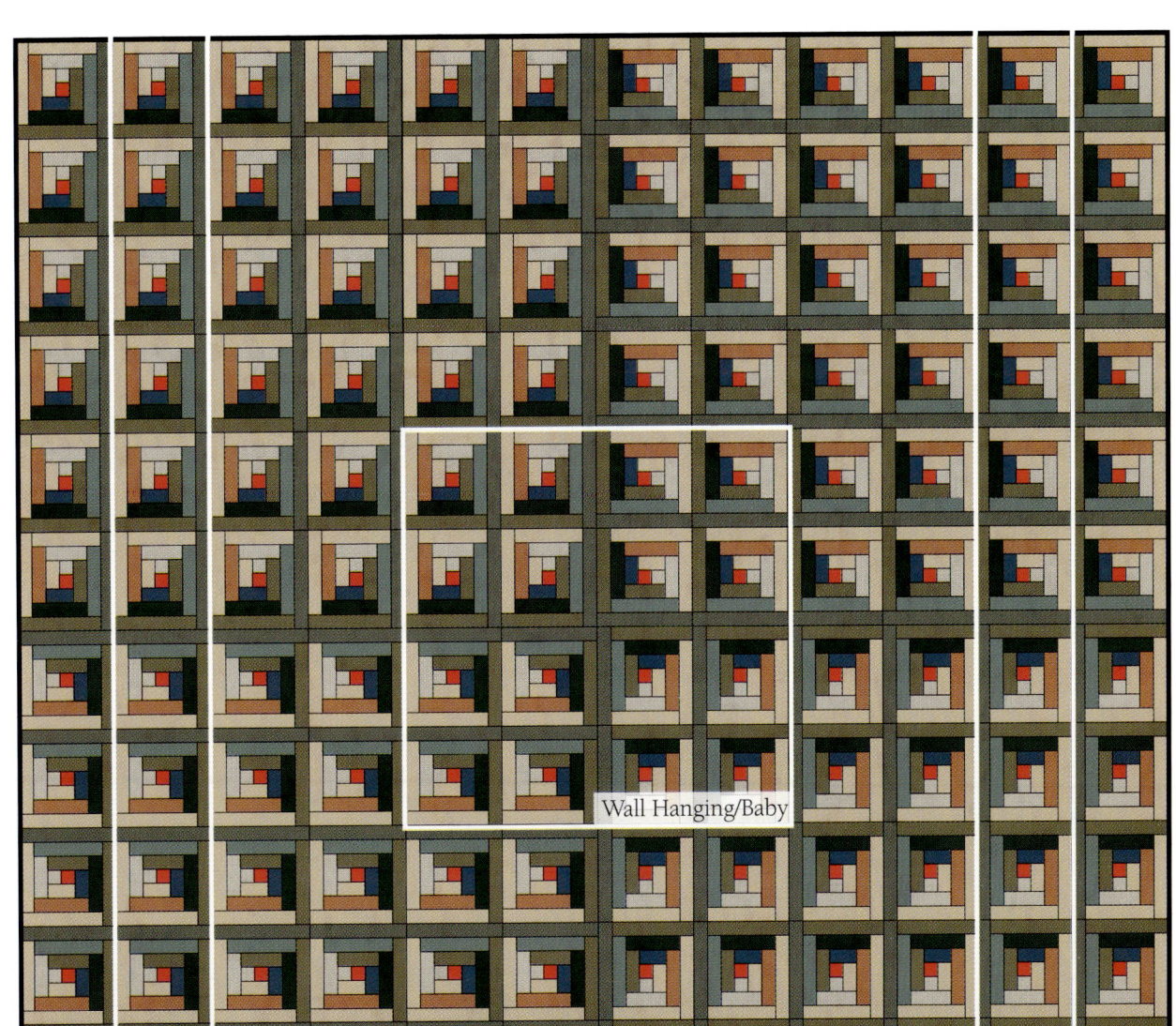

Layout for Other Sizes

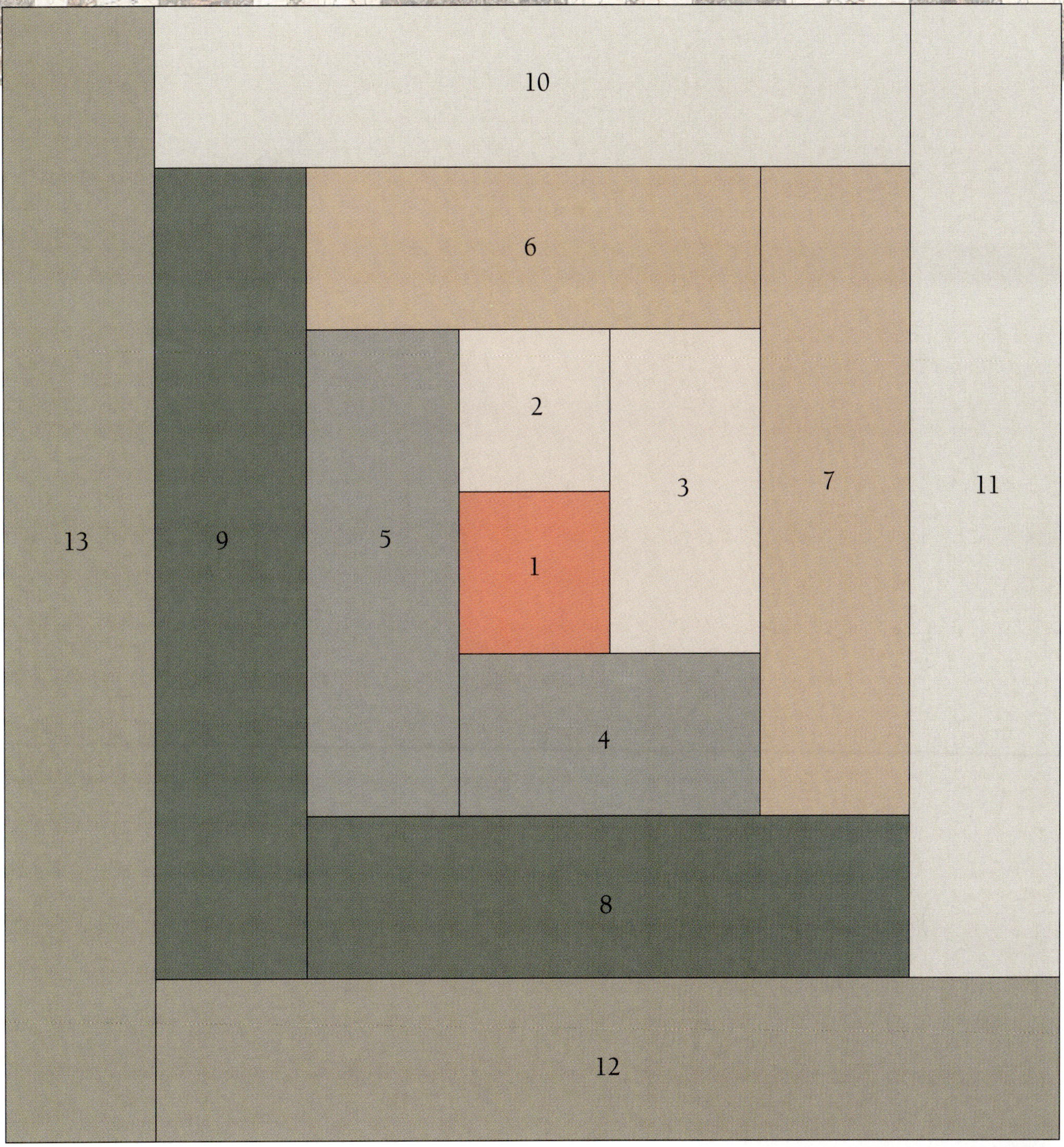

Rose Garden Block

Block Diagram

23

Baby Stars

Approximate Size: 35" x 42"
Baby/Wall hanging Setting: 4 x 5
Number of Blocks: 20

Materials

Note: The fabric amounts given are based on what is needed for this project. Due to flannel shrinkage, you may want to purchase at least ¼ to ½ yd more of each fabric.

¼ yd gold
⅜ yd lavender
⅜ yd green
⅜ yd blue floral 1
½ yd blue floral 2
⅝ yd blue floral 3
⅞ yd dk floral print
¾ yd lt blue border
⅜ yd binding
Crib-size batting
1¼ yds backing

Cutting Requirements

Note: All strips include ½" seam allowance.
Cut the following 2"-wide strips for piecing:
Two strips, gold
Four strips, lavender
Five strips, green
Five strips, blue floral 1
Eight strips, blue floral 2
Eleven strips, blue floral 3
One strips, dk floral

Cut the following 5"-wide strips for piecing:
Three strips, dk floral (Cut into 5" squares, then cut in half diagonally for triangles.)

Cut the following 5"-wide strips border:
Three strips, dk floral (Cut into 5" squares. Do NOT cut into triangles.)

Five strips, lt blue (Cut into 18 rectangles, 5" x 8" and four 5" squares.)

Cut the following binding strips:
Five 2"-wide strips, binding

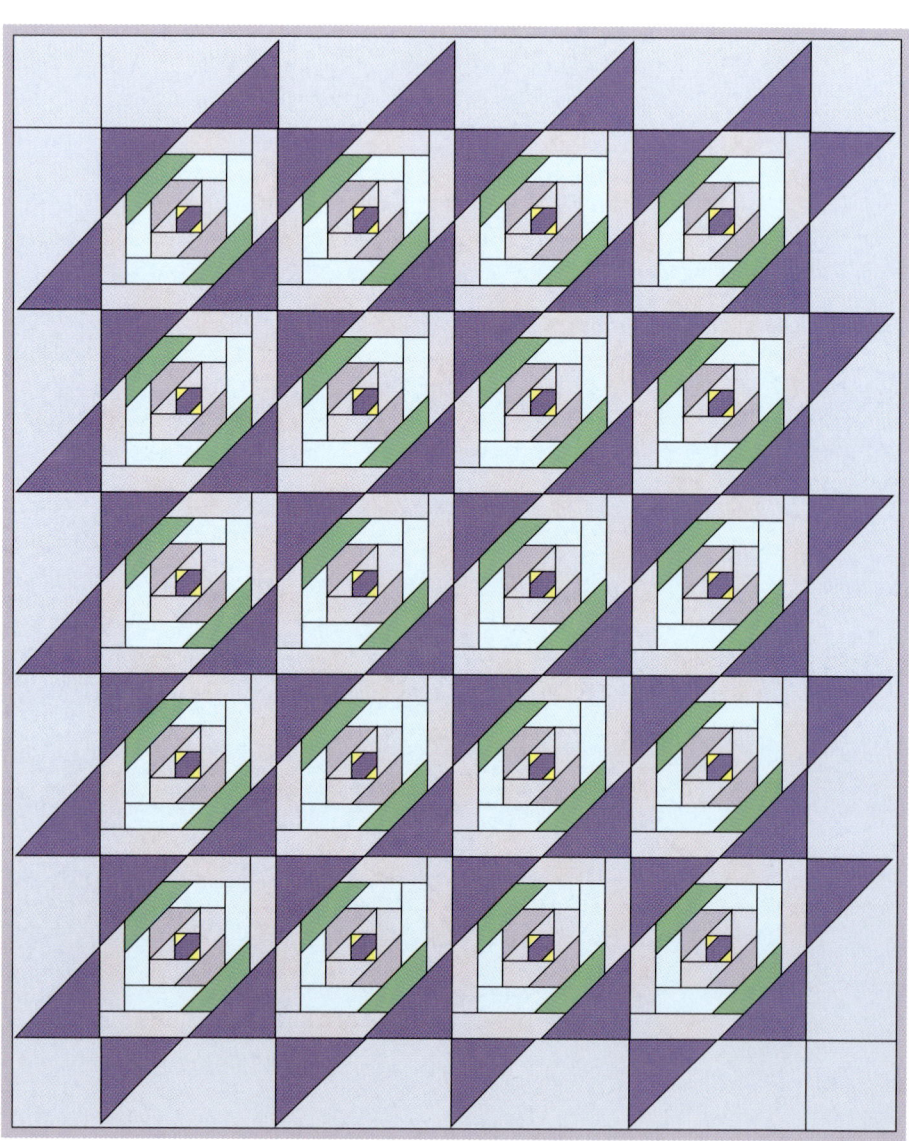

Quilt Diagram

Continued on page 26

Instructions

Note: Read Working with Flannel: an Overview, page 4 before beginning. Use a ½" seam allowance for sewing.

1. Refer to How to Make a Foundation-Pieced Block, pages 6 to 9, and make 20 Log Cabin blocks using pattern on page 29.
2. Arrange blocks in five rows of four blocks according to photograph.
3. Sew blocks together in rows; then sew rows together. Press seams in alternate directions.
4. For border, place a dk floral square right sides together with lt blue rectangle, **Fig 1**. Sew diagonally from outside corner, **Fig 2**. **Hint:** Fold square in half or draw a pencil line diagonally for a sewing guide, **Fig 3**.

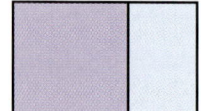

Fig 1

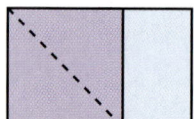

Fig 2

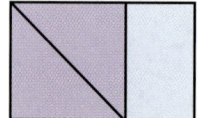

Fig 3

5. Trim ½" from sewing line, **Fig 4**, then fold dk floral fabric over seam allowance; press.

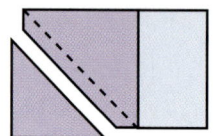

Fig 4

6. Repeat steps 4 and 5 for a total of eight pieced rectangles with triangles on the right and 10 pieced triangles with triangles on the left, **Fig 5**.

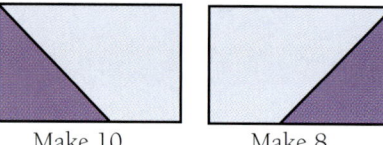

Make 10   Make 8

Fig 5

7. Sew together five pieced rectangles (with triangles on the left), **Fig 6**; repeat. Sew to sides of quilt top.
8. Sew four pieced rectangles (with triangles on the right), **Fig 7**; repeat. Then, sew a 5" square on each end of both strips. Sew to top and bottom of quilt, **Fig 8**.
9. Finish quilt referring to Finishing Your Quilt, pages 9 to 11.

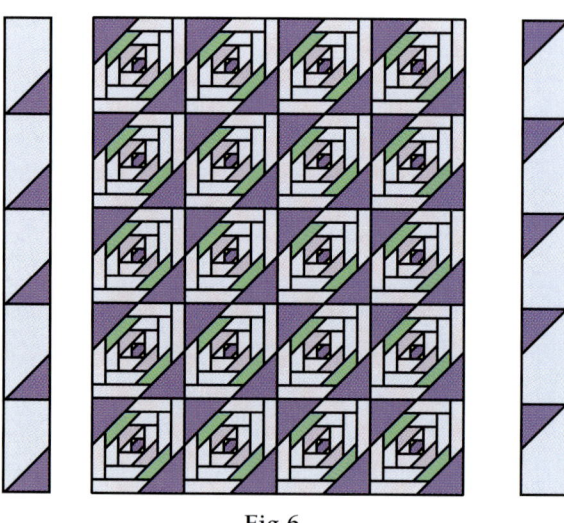

Fig 6

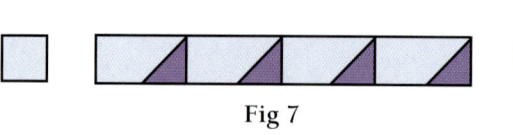

Fig 7

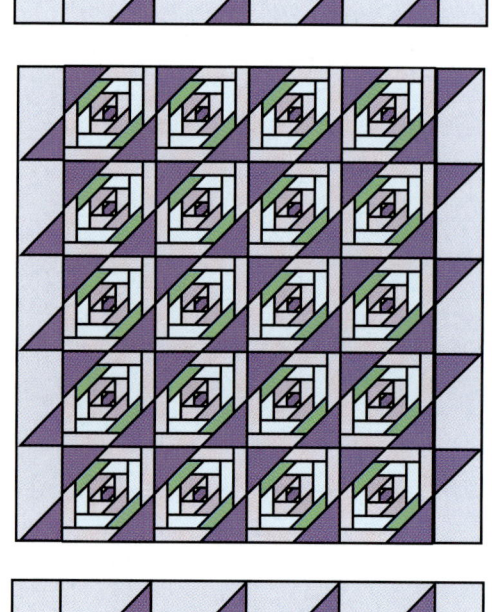

Fig 8

Other Sizes

The following chart shows number of strips needed to make the number of Log Cabin blocks for five other quilt sizes. Strips are cut 2"-wide unless otherwise noted.

	Lap	Twin	Full	Queen	King
Size	49" x 63"	75" x 89"	82" x 96"	96" x 103"	103" x 103"
Setting	6 x 8	8 x 10	9 x 11	11 x 12	12 x 12
Blocks	48	80	99	132	144
Gold	5	7	9	12	13
Lavender	10	16	20	27	29
Green	12	20	25	33	36
Blue floral 1	12	20	25	33	36
Blue floral 2	20	32	40	53	57
Blue floral 3	24	40	50	66	72
Dk floral (center)	3	4	5	7	8
Dk floral (triangles)	6 @ 5" wide	10 @ 5" wide	14 @ 5" wide	17 @ 5" wide	18 @ 5" wide
Dk floral (border squares)	4 @ 5" wide	5 @ 5" wide	5 @ 5" wide	6 @ 5" wide	6 @ 5" wide
Lt blue	7 @ 5" wide	9 @ 5" wide	9 @ 5" wide	10 @ 5" wide	11 @ 5" wide
Binding	6	9	10	10	11

Note: The widths are the cut measurements.

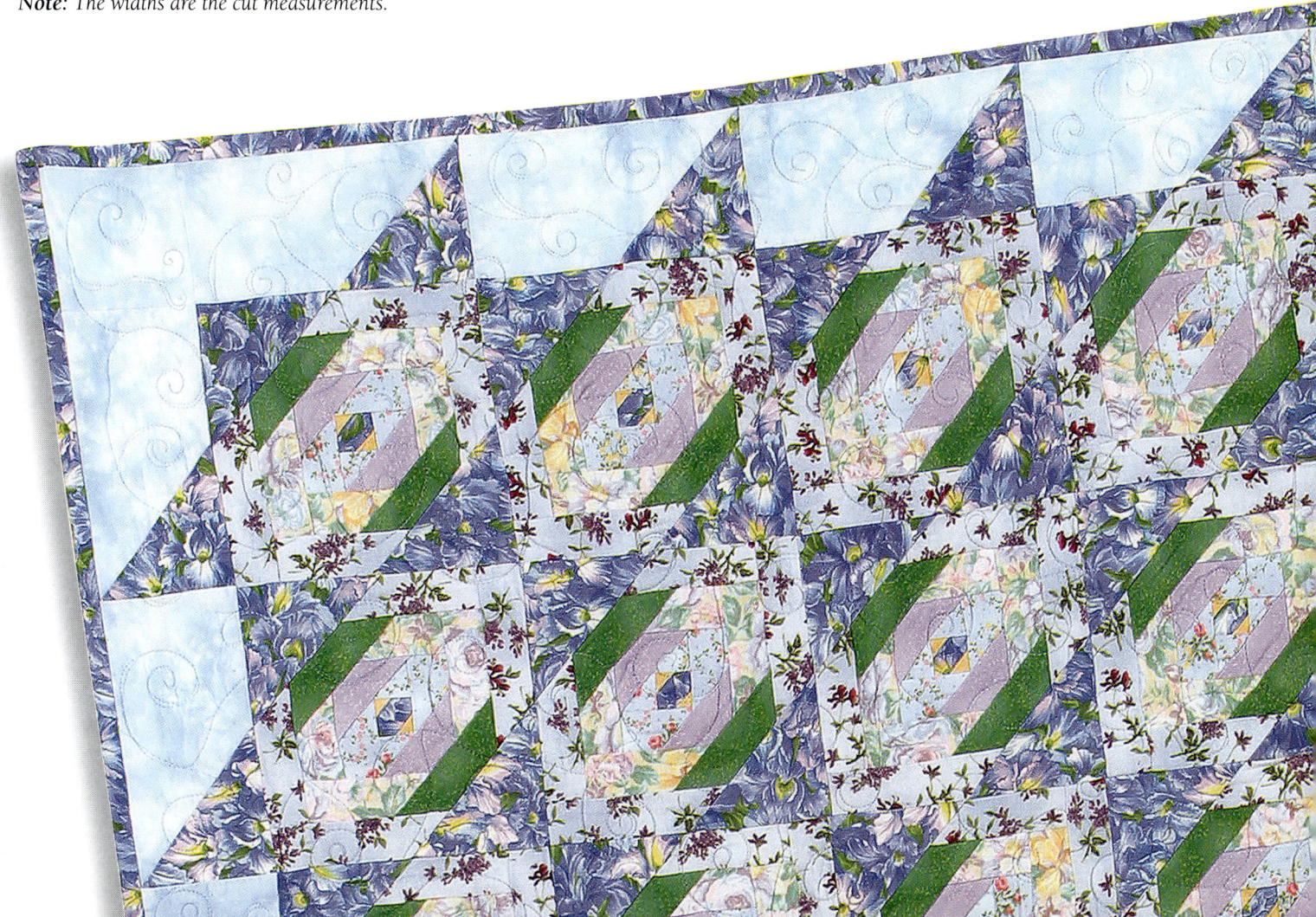

The following chart shows the yardage needed for each size quilt. Purchase ¼ to ½ yd more to allow for flannel shrinkage.

Yardage	Lap	Twin	Full	Queen	King
Gold	⅜ yd	½ yd	½ yd	¾ yd	¾ yd
Lavender	⅝ yd	1 yd	1⅜ yds	1⅝ yds	1¾ yds
Green	¾ yd	1¼ yds	1½ yds	1⅞ yds	2⅛ yds
Blue Floral 1	¾ yd	1¼ yds	1½ yds	1⅞ yds	2½ yds
Blue floral 2	1¼ yds	1⅞ yds	2⅜ yds	3 yds	3¼ yds
Blue floral 3	1⅜ yds	2¼ yds	2⅞ yds	3¾ yds	4⅛ yds
Dk floral	1⅝ yds	2⅜ yds	3 yds	3¾ yds	3⅞ yds
Lt blue	1 yd	1⅜ yds	1⅜ yds	1½ yds	1⅝ yds
Binding	⅜ yd	⅝ yd	⅝ yd	⅝ yd	¾ yd

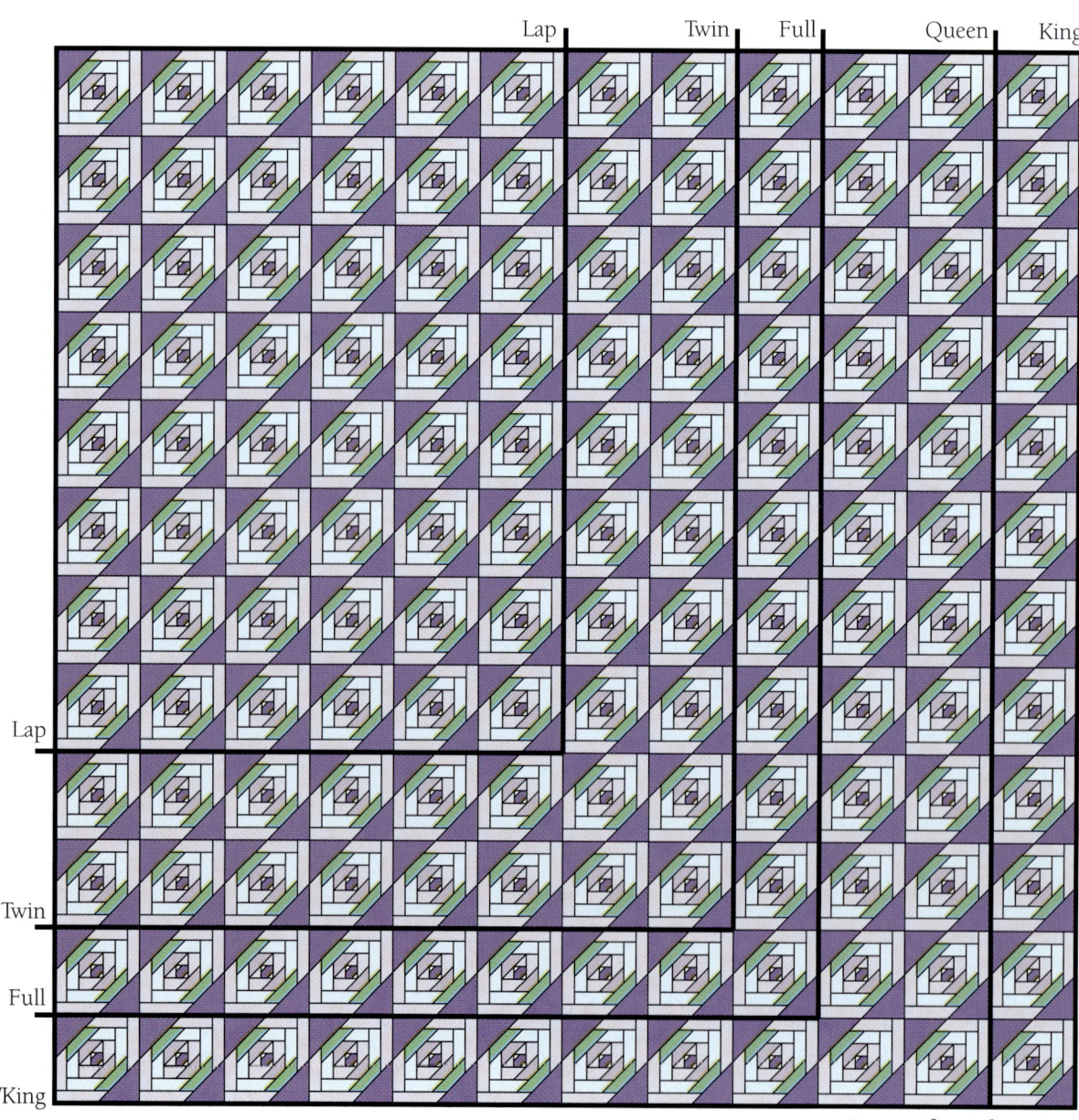

Layout for Other Sizes

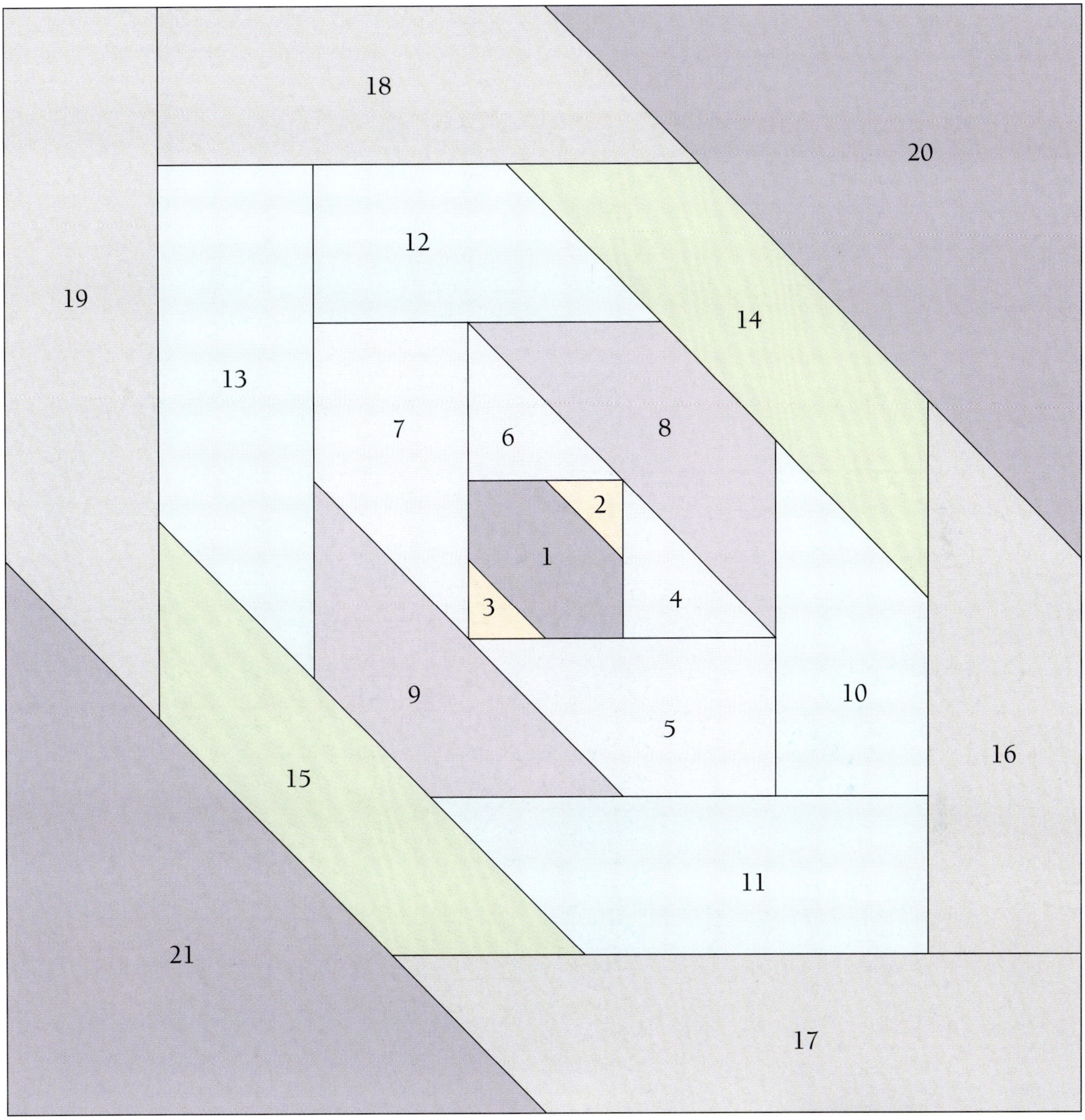

Star Galaxy Block

Block Diagram

29

Rainbow Clamshells

Approximate Size: 56" x 70"
Lap Size Setting: 6 x 8
Number of Blocks: 52
(includes corner blocks for border)

Materials

⅜ yd purple
¼ yd red
⅜ yd pink
½ yd orange
⅝ yd green
½ yd blue
⅛ yd black 1 (centers)
⅞ yd black print 2
⅞ yd black print 3
⅞ yd black print 4
1¼ yds border print
⅜ yd binding fabric
3½ yds backing
twin-size batting

Cutting Requirements

Note: All strips include ½" seam allowance.

Cut the following 2¼" squares for centers:
Two squares, red
Three squares, pink
Five squares, orange
Six squares, green
Five squares, blue
Three squares, purple
28 squares, black 1

Cut the following 1¼"-wide strips for piecing:
Two strips, purple
Three strips, red
Five strips, pink
Five strips, orange
Five strips, green
Three strips, blue
Six strips, black print 2
Six strips, black print 3
Six strips, black print 4

Cut the following 2¼"-wide strips for piecing:
Three strips, purple
Two strips, red
Three strips, pink
Five strips, orange
Six strips, green
Five strips, blue
Eight strips, black print 2
Eight strips, black print 3
Eight strips, black print 4

Cut the following border and binding strips:
Five 8"-wide strips, border
Seven 2"-wide strips, binding

Quilt Diagram

Continued on page 32

Instructions

Note: Read Working with Flannel: An Overview, page 4 before beginning.

1. Refer to How to Make a Foundation-Pieced Block, pages 6 to 8, and make 52 Log Cabin blocks using pattern on page 35 and referring to deagrams on page 34 for various color placements.
2. Arrange blocks in eight rows of six blocks according to photograph (or your own desired layout).
3. Sew blocks together in rows; then sew rows together. Press seams in alternate directions.
4. Measure quilt top lengthwise; piece 8"-wide border strips to achieve needed length (refer to Making a Quilt Top, page 8, for piecing border strips); repeat for another strip. Sew strips to opposite sides of quilt top. Press seams toward border.
5. Measure quilt top crosswise; piece 3"-wide border strips to achieve needed length; repeat for another strip. Sew a Log cabin block to short ends of each border strip, referring to quilt layout on page 30. Sew strips to top and bottom of quilt top. Press seams toward border.
6. Finish quilt referring to Finishing Your Quilt, pages 9 to 11.

Other Sizes

The following chart shows number of strips needed to make the number of Log Cabin blocks for five other quilt sizes.

	Wall hanging/Baby	Twin	Full	Queen	King
Size	42" x 42"	70" x 94"	84" x 98"	92" x 106"	106" x 106"
Setting	4 x 4	8 x 12	10 x 12	10 x 12	12 x 12
Blocks (includes corners)	20	100	124	124	148
Purple	1 @ 1¼"	7 @ 1¼" 9 @ 2¼"	9 @ 1¼" 10 @ 2¼"	9 @ 1¼" 11 @ 2¼"	10 @ 1¼" 12 @ 2¼"
Red	3 @ 1¼" 1 @ 2¼"	6 @ 1¼" 8 @ 2¼"	7 @ 1¼" 10 @ 2¼"	8 @ 1¼" 10 @ 2¼"	10 @ 1¼" 11 @ 2¼"
Pink	4 @ 1¼" 3 @ 2¼"	6 @ 1¼" 8 @ 2¼"	7 @ 1¼" 10 @ 2¼"	7 @ 1¼" 10 @ 2¼"	10 @ 1¼" 11 @ 2¼"
Orange	1 @ 1¼" 3 @ 2¼"	6 @ 1¼" 8 @ 2¼"	7 @ 1¼" 10 @ 2¼"	8 @ 1¼" 10 @ 2¼"	10 @ 1¼" 11 @ 2¼"
Green	1 @ 2¼"	7 @ 1¼" 8 @ 2¼"	8 @ 1¼" 10 @ 2¼"	8 @ 1¼" 10 @ 2¼"	10 @ 1¼" 11 @ 2¼"
Blue	2 @ 1¼"	7 @ 1¼" 8 @ 2¼"	8 @ 1¼" 10 @ 2¼"	8 @ 1¼" 10 @ 2¼"	10 @ 1¼" 11 @ 2¼"
Black 1	2 @ 2¼"	3 @ 2¼"	4 @ 2¼"	4 @ 2¼"	5 @ 2¼"
Black 2	2 @ 1¼" 4 @ 2¼"	12 @ 1¼" 15 @ 2¼"	14 @ 1¼" 18 @ 2¼"	14 @ 1¼" 18 @ 2¼"	17 @ 1¼" 22 @ 2¼"
Black 3	3 @ 1¼" 4 @ 2¼"	13 @ 1¼" 15 @ 2¼"	16 @ 1¼" 18 @ 2¼"	16 @ 1¼" 18 @ 2¼"	18 @ 1¼" 22 @ 2¼"
Black 4	3 @ 1¼" 4 @ 2¼"	16 @ 1¼" 18 @ 2¼"	21 @ 1¼" 21 @ 2¼"	21 @ 1¼" 21 @ 2¼"	25 @ 1¼" 25 @ 2¼"
Border 1	4 @ 8" wide	9 @ 8" wide	10 @ 8"	10 @ 5"	11 @ 5"
Border 2	-	-	-	11 @ 8"	12 @ 8" wide
Binding	5 @ 2" wide	9 @ 2" wide	9 @ 2" wide	11 @ 2" wide	12 @ 2" wide

Note: The border widths are the cut measurements.

The following chart shows the yardage needed for each size quilt.

Yardage	Baby	Twin	Full	Queen	King
Purple	⅛ yd	⅞ yd	1 yd	1 yd	1⅛ yds
Red	¼ yd	¾ yd	⅞ yd	1 yd	1⅛ yds
Pink	¾ yd	¾ yd	⅞ yd	1 yd	1⅛ yds
Orange	1¼ yds	¾ yd	⅞ yd	1 yd	1⅛ yds
Green	⅛ yd	¾ yd	⅞ yd	1 yd	1⅛ yds
Blue	1⅛ yds	¾ yd	⅞ yd	1 yd	1⅛ yds
Black 1	⅛ yd	⅜ yd	3½ yd	3½ yd	⅝ yd
Black 2	⅜ yd	1½ yds	1¾ yds	2⅛ yds	2 yds
Black 3	⅜ yd	1½ yds	1¾ yds	2⅛ yds	2⅛ yds
Black 4	⅜ yd	1¾ yds	2⅛ yds	2⅛ yds	2½ yds
Border 1	1 yd	2 yds	2¼ yds	1½ yds	1⅝ yds
Border 2	-	-	-	2½ yds	2¾ yds
Binding	⅜ yd	½ yd	½ yd	⅝ yd	¾ yd
Backing	2 yds	5½ yds	7½ yds	8 yds	9¼ yds

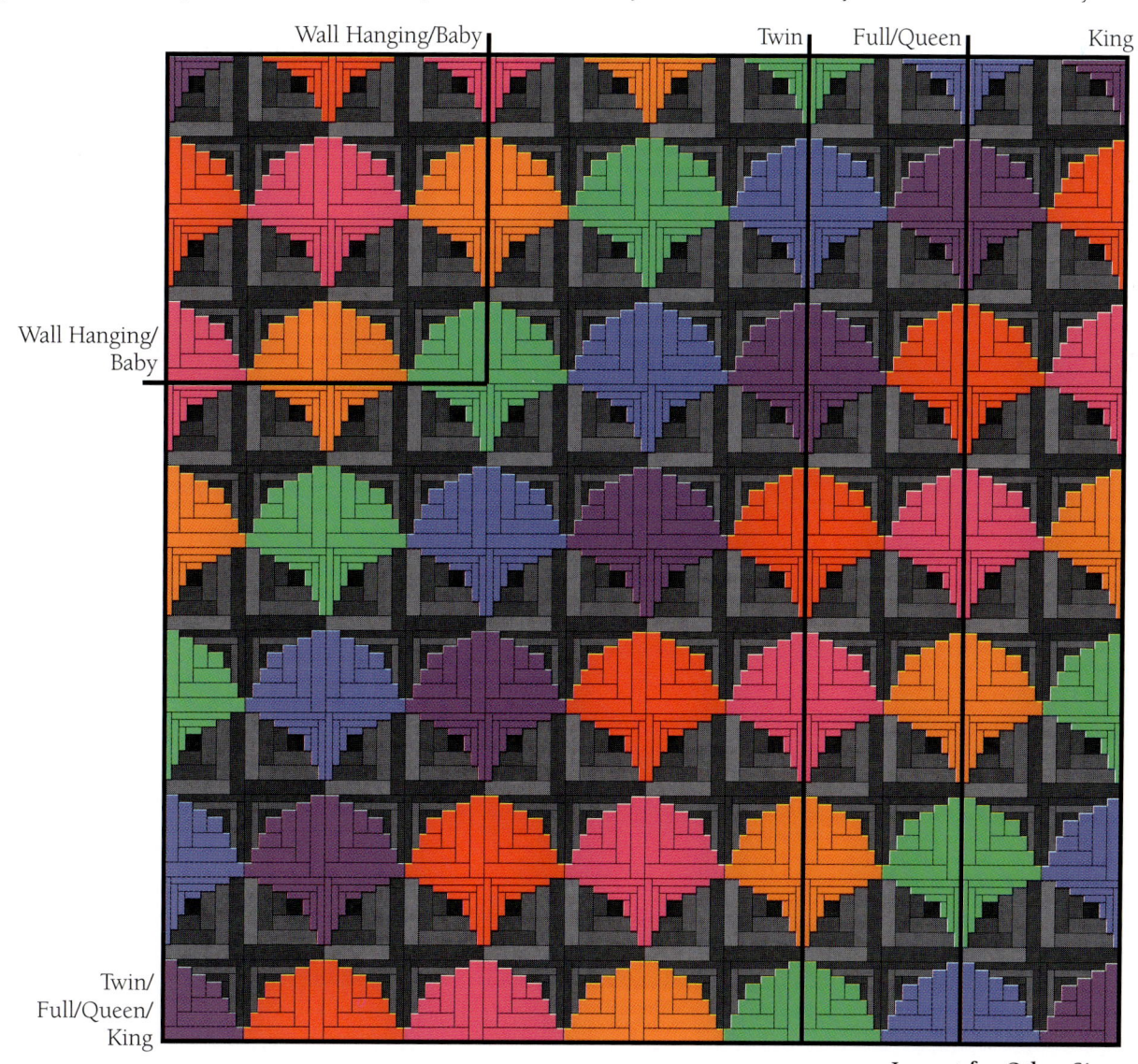

Layout for Other Sizes

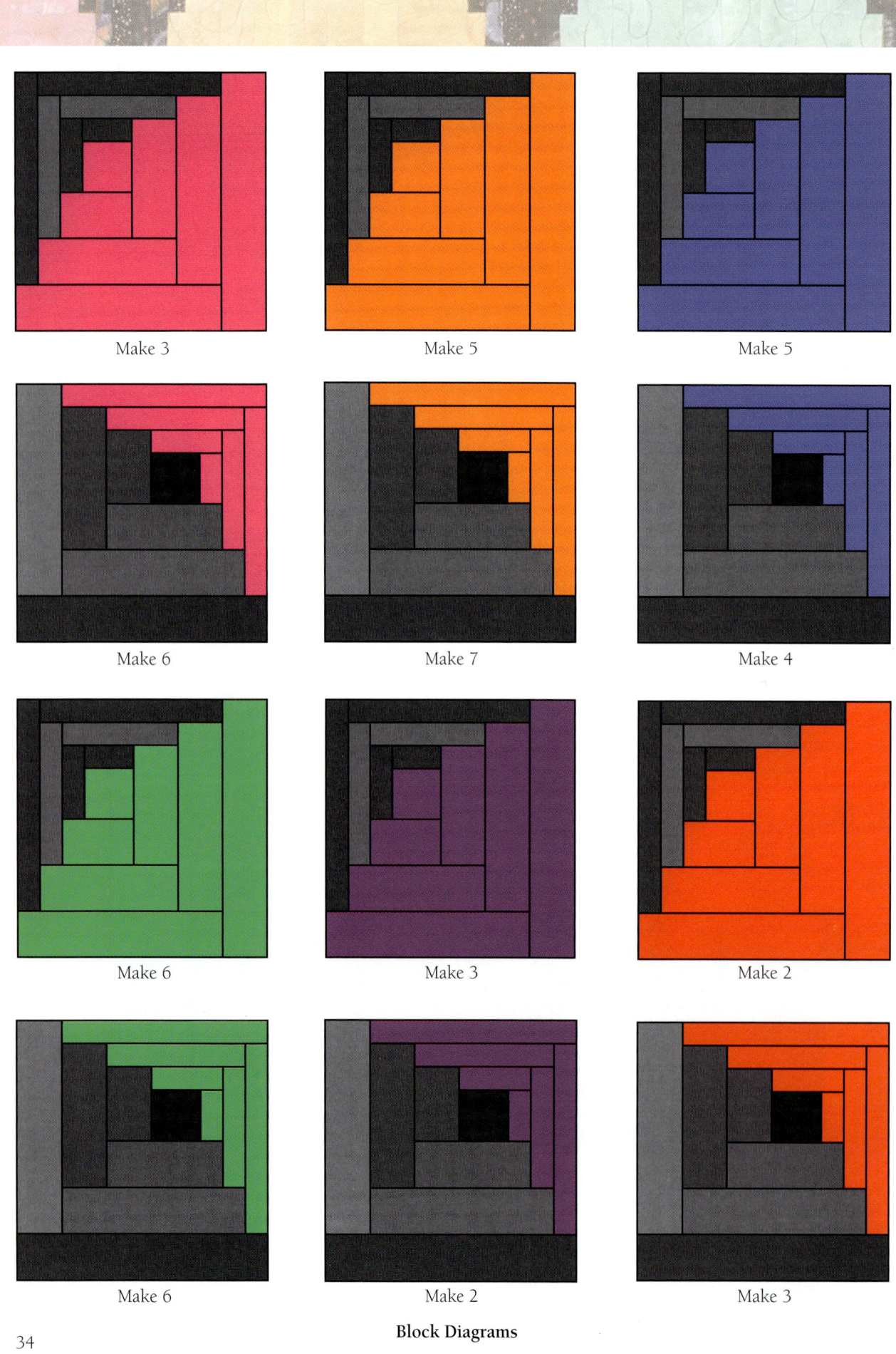

Block Diagrams

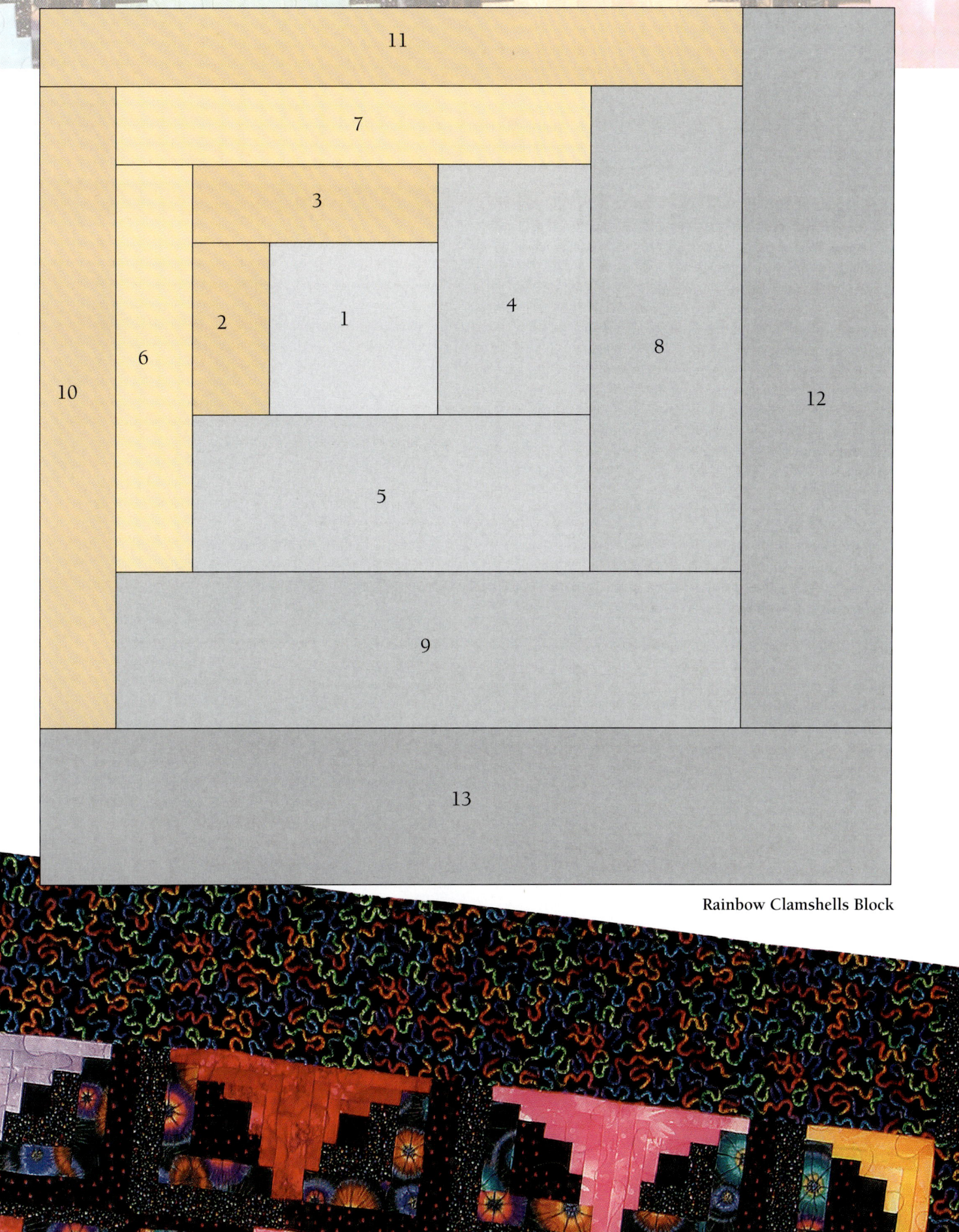

Rainbow Clamshells Block

Star Galaxy

Approximate Size: 52" x 66"
Lap Size Setting: 6 x 8
Number of Blocks: 48

Materials

Note: The fabric amounts given are based on what is needed for this project. Due to flannel shrinkage, you may want to purchase at least ¼ to ½ yd more of each fabric.

2 yds star print (includes border)
1½ yds lt blue
2 yds med blue (includes binding)
1 yd dk blue
1½ yds yellow
1¼ yds gold
⅞ yd rust
3½ yds backing
twin-size batting

Cutting Requirements

Note: All strips include ½" seam allowance.

Cut the following 2"-wide strips for piecing:
20 strips lt blue (logs 10,11)
18 strips med blue (logs 6,7)
15 strips dk blue (logs 2,3)
13 strips, rust (logs 4,5)

Cut the following 2½"-wide strips for piecing:
20 strips yellow (logs 12, 13)
16 strips gold (logs 8, 9)

Cut the following 4½"-wide strips for centers:
Six strips, star print

Cut the following border and binding strips:
Six 6"-wide strips, border
Seven 2"-wide strips, binding

Instructions

Note: Read Working with Flannel: An Overview, page 4 before beginning.

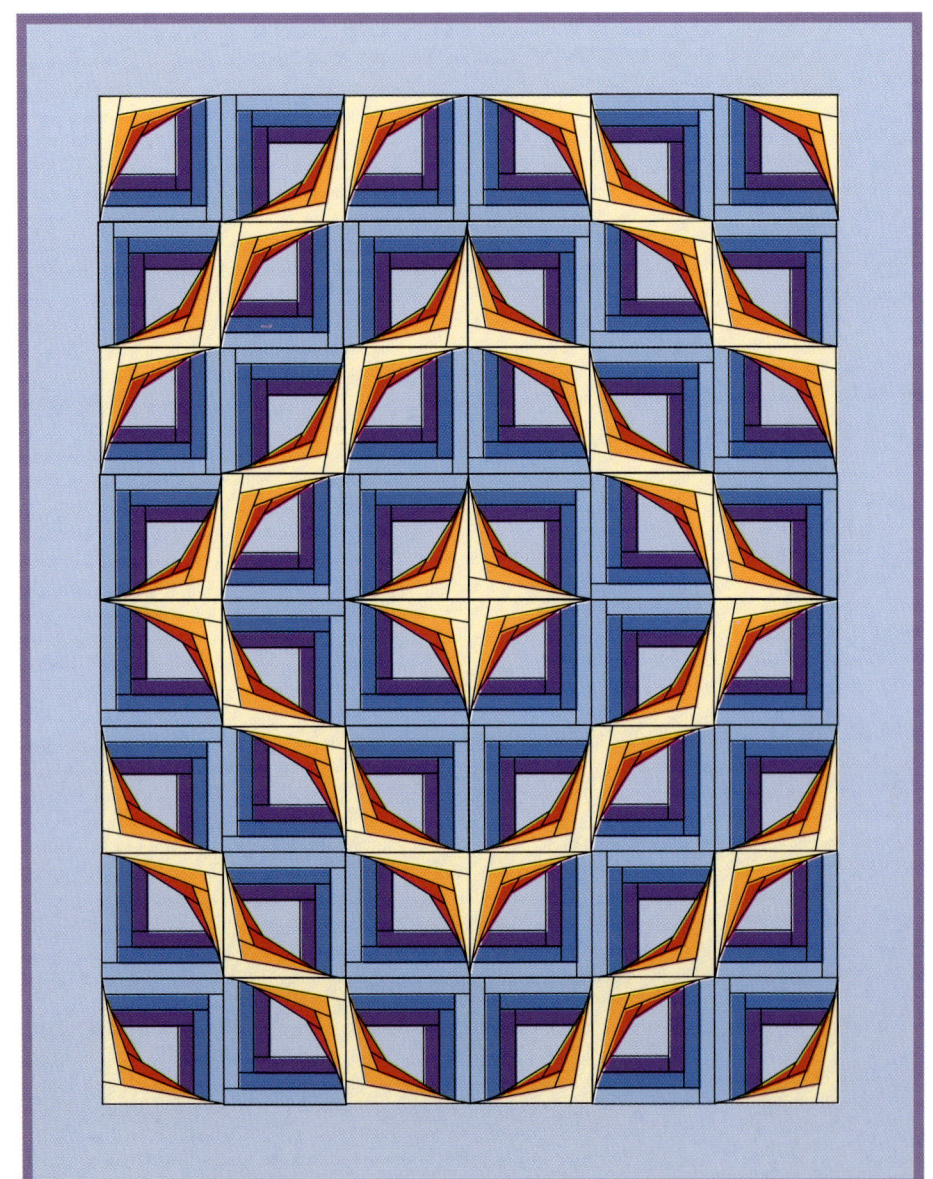

Quilt Diagram

1. Refer to How to Make a Foundation-Pieced Block, pages 6 to 8, and make 48 Log Cabin blocks using pattern on page 41.

2. Arrange blocks in eight rows of six blocks according to photograph (or your own desired layout).

Continued on page 38

3. Sew blocks together in rows; then sew rows together. Press seams in alternate directions.
4. Measure quilt top lengthwise; piece 3"-wide border strips to achieve needed length (refer to Making a Quilt Top, page 8, for piecing border strips); repeat for another strip. Sew strips to opposite sides of quilt top. Press seams toward border.
5. Measure quilt top crosswise, including borders just added; piece 3"-wide border strips to achieve needed length; repeat for another strip. Sew strips to top and bottom of quilt top. Press seams toward border.
6. Finish quilt referring to Finishing Your Quilt, pages 9 to 11.

Other Sizes

The following chart shows number of strips or squares needed to make the number of Log Cabin blocks for five other quilt sizes. Strips are cut 2" unless otherwise noted.

	Wall hanging/Baby	Twin	Full	Queen	King
Size	40" x 40'	68" x 89"	78" x 99"	94" x 100"	104" x 104"
Setting	4 x 4	8 x 11	8 x 11	10 x 11	12 x 12
Blocks	16	88	88	110	144
Center Square strips	2 @ 4½"	11 @ 4½"	11 @ 4½"	14 @ 4½"	18 @ 4½"
Dk blue strips	5	25	25	31	40
Med blue strips	5	30	30	37	48
Lt blue strips	7	34	34	42	55
Rust strips	5	23	23	28	37
Gold strips	6 @ 2¼" wide	28 @ 2¼"	28 @ 2¼"	35 @ 2¼"	46 @ 2¼"
Yellow strips	7 @ 2¼" wide	35 @ 2¼"	35 @ 2¼"	43 @ 2¼"	56 @ 2¼"
Border 1	4 @ 3" wide	7 @ 3" wide	7 @ 3" wide	8 @ 4" wide	9 @ 4" wide
Border 2	4 @ 5" wide	8 @ 5" wide	7 @ 3" wide	8 @ 3" wide	10 @ 8" wide
Border 3	-	-	8 @ 7" wide	9 @ 8" wide	-
Binding	5 @ 3" wide	8 @ 3" wide	9 @ 3" wide	10 @ 3" wide	11 @ 3" wide

Note: The border widths are the cut measurements.

The following chart shows the yardage needed for each size quilt.

Yardage

Center Square strips	¼ yd	1½ yds	1½ yds	1⅞ yds	2⅜ yds
Logs 2, 3 strips	⅜ yd	1½ yds	1½ yds	1⅞ yds	2⅜ yds
Logs 4, 5 strips	⅓ yd	1½ yds	1½ yds	1¾ yds	2⅜ yds
Logs 6, 7 strips	⅜ yd	1¾ yds	1¾ yds	2⅛ yds	2⅞ yds
Logs 8, 9 strips	½ yd	1¾ yds	1¾ yds	2½ yds	3½ yds
Logs 10, 11 strips	½ yd	2 yds	2 yds	2½ yds	3¼ yds
Logs 12, 13 strips	½ yd	2½ yds	2½ yds	3⅛ yds	4 yds
Border 1	⅜ yd	⅝ yd	⅝ yd	1 yd	1⅛ yds
Border 2	⅝ yd	1¼ yds	½ yd	¾ yd	2⅜ yds
Border 3	-	-	1¾ yds	2⅛ yds	-
Binding	½ yd	¾ yd	⅞ yd	1 yd	1 yd

Layout for Other Sizes

39

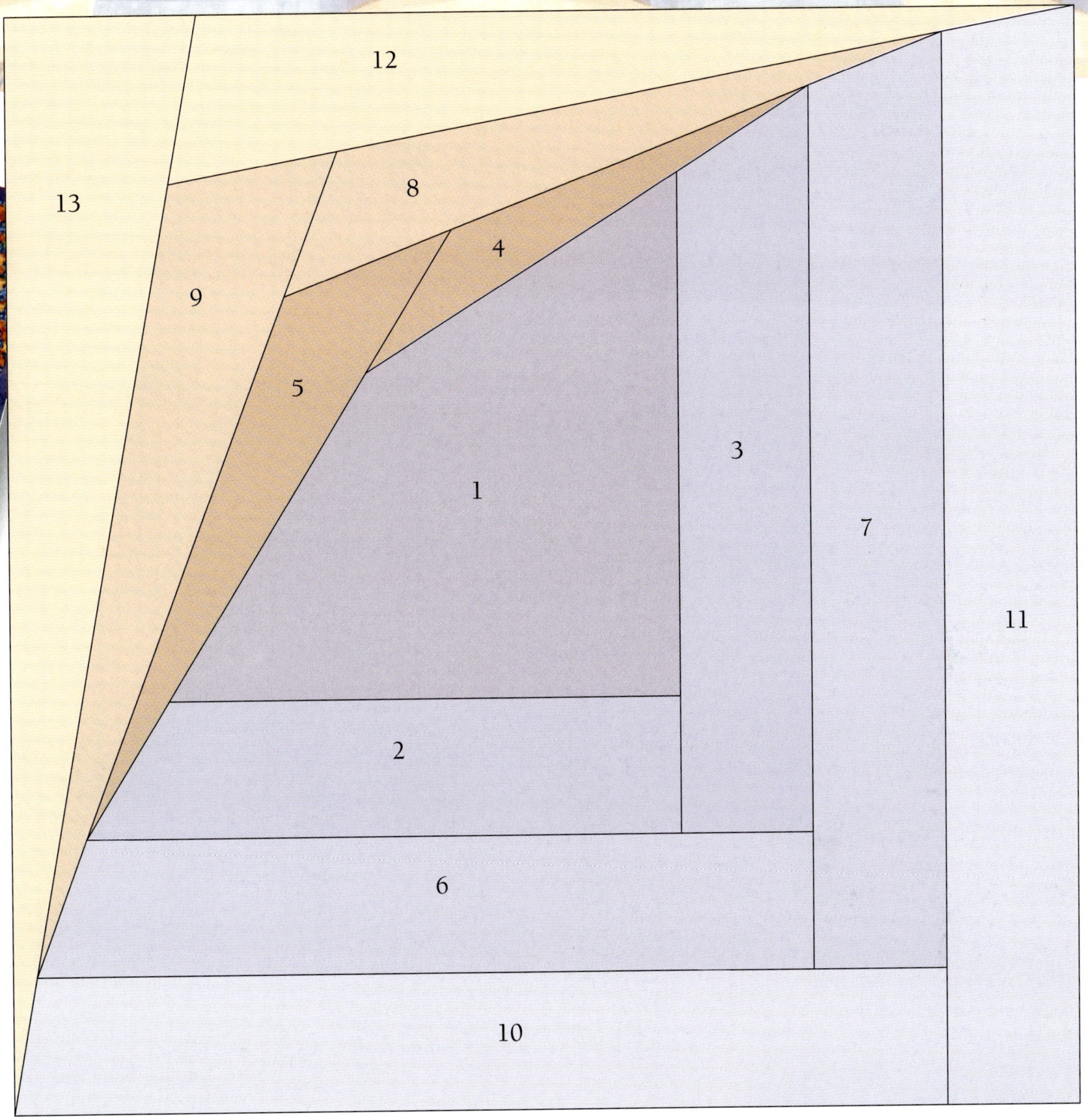

Star Galaxy Block

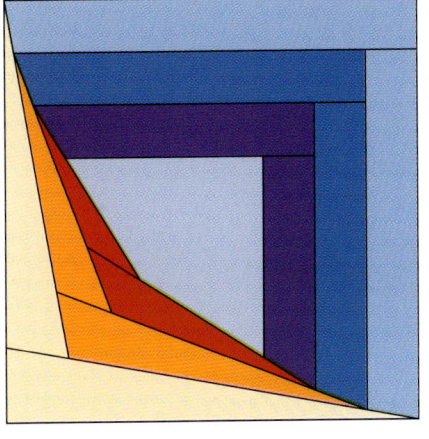

Block Diagram

41

Baby Pinwheels

Approximate Size: 37½" x 37½"
Baby Quilt Size Setting: 4 x 4
Number of Blocks: eight Block 1, eight Block 2

Materials

¼ yd lt letter print
⅓ yd lt dot print
⅜ yd lt cloud print
¾ yd dk blue (includes sashing)
⅜ yd dk green
½ yd dk pink
1 yd lt green animal print (border and binding)
1½ yds backing
Crib-size batting

Cutting Requirements

Note: All strips include ½" seam allowance.

Cut the following 2"-wide strips for piecing:

Block 1
Eight 4" x 4" squares (fussy cut for centers)
Two 2"-wide strips, lt letter print
Two 2"-wide strips, lt dot print
Two 2"-wide strips, lt cloud print
Three 2"-wide strips, dk green
Four 2"-wide strips, dk pink

Block 2
One 2"-wide strips, lt letter print
Two 2"-wide strips, lt dot print
Three 2"-wide strips, lt cloud print
Three 2"-wide strips, dk blue
Two 2"-wide strips, dk green
Three 2"-wide strips, dk pink

Cut the following 2"-wide strips for sashing:
Six 2"-wide strips, dk blue

Wall Hanging/Baby Quilt Layout

Cut the following border and binding strips:
Four 4¼"-wide strips, lt green animal print (border)
Four 2"-wide strips, lt green animal print (binding)

Instructions

Note: Read Working with Flannel: An Overview, page 4 before beginning.

1. Refer to How to Make a Foundation-Pieced Block, pages 6 to 8, and make eight Log Cabin 1 blocks and eight Log Cabin 2 blocks using patterns on page 47 and 48.
2. Arrange blocks in four rows of four blocks according to Quilt Layout above. Note that the two middle rows form two pinwheels.
3. For first row, sew blocks in pairs. Cut a 2" x 8" dk blue sashing strip, then sew between pairs of blocks; press seams toward sashing strip. Repeat for fourth row.

Continued on page 44

4. For second and third rows, sew blocks in pairs, then sew pairs together to form two pinwheels (see photo at top left of page 42). Measure pinwheel and cut a 2"-wide dk blue sashing strip to that length (it should measure 15"). Sew sashing strip between pinwheels; press toward sashing strip.

5. Measure all rows crosswise and cut two 2"-wide dk blue sashing strips to that length (they should measure 30"). Sew rows and sashing strips together; press toward sashing strips.

6. Measure quilt top lengthwise; cut two 2"-wide dk blue sashing strips to that length. Sew to sides of quilt. Press seams toward dk blue strips.

7. Measure quilt top crosswise, including strips just added; cut two 2"-wide dk blue sashing strips to that length. Sew to top and bottom of quilt top. Press seams toward dk blue strips.

8. Repeat steps 6 and 7 for border using 4¼"-wide animal print strips.

9. Finish quilt referring to Finishing Your Quilt, pages 9 to 11.

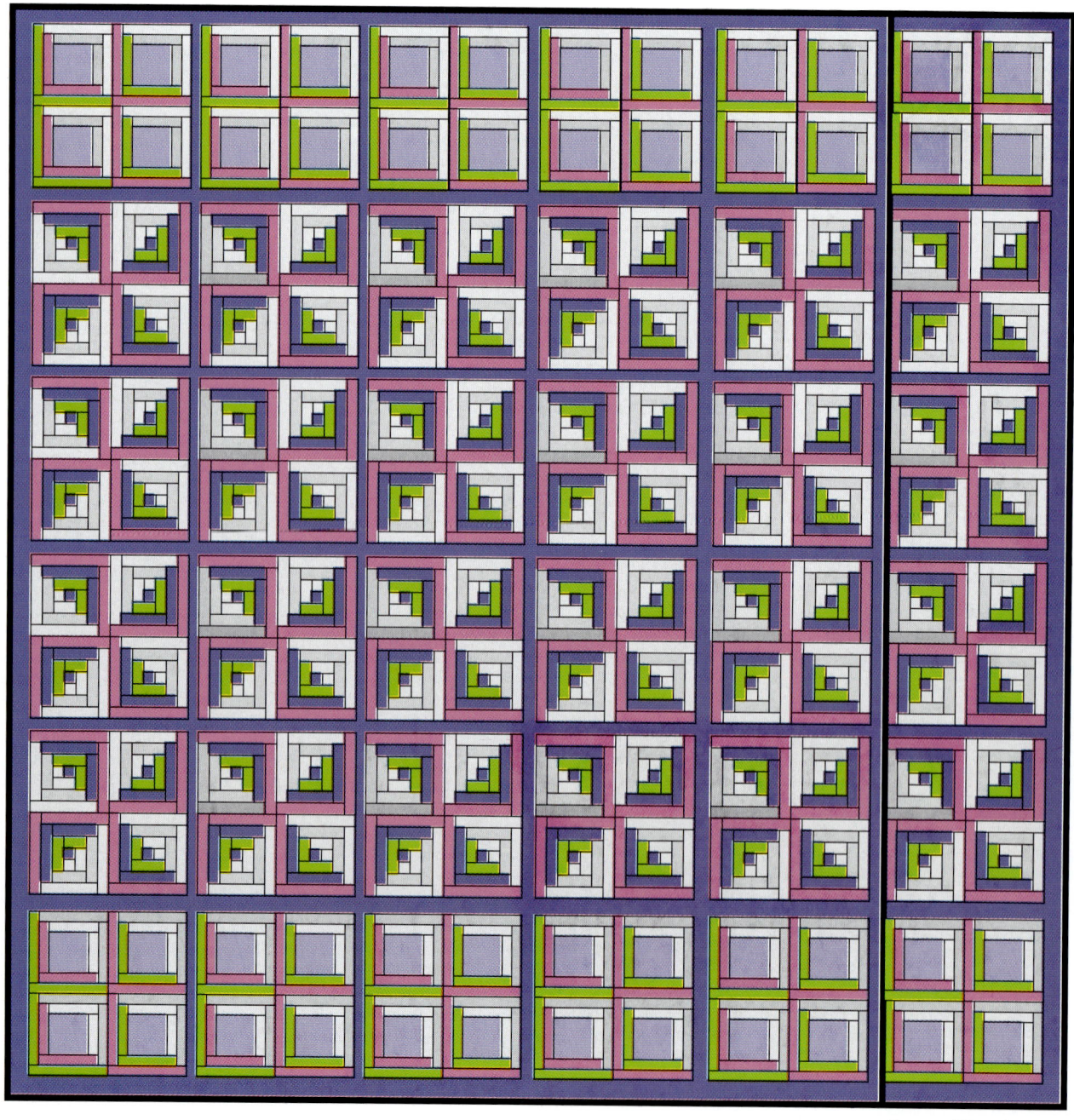

Queen/King Layout

Other Sizes

The following chart shows number of strips or squares needed to make the number of Log Cabin blocks for five other quilt sizes. Strips are cut 2" unless otherwise noted.

	Lap	Twin	Full	Queen	King
Size	56" x 72"	73" x 89"	80" x 98"	92" x 106"	106" x 106"
Setting	6 x 8	8 x 10	8 x 10	10 x 12	12 x 12
Blocks	12 Block 1	32 Block 1	32 Block 1	40 Block 1	48 Block 1
	36 Block 2	48 block 2	48 block 2	80 block 2	96 Block 2
Animal print squares	12 @ 4" x 4"	32 @ 4" x 4"	32 @ 4" x 4"	40 @ 4" x 4"	48 @ 4" x 4"
Lt letter print strips	7	13	13	17	22
Lt dot print strips	11	17	17	25	31
Lt cloud print strips	17	25	25	35	43
Dk blue strips	13	17	17	26	32
Dk green strips	14	21	21	28	35
Dk pink strips	20	31	31	44	54
Sashing	14 @ 2" wide	22 @ 2" wide	23 @ 3" wide	20 @ 3" wide	26 @ 3" wide
Border	7 @ 6" wide	8 @ 7" wide	9 @ 8" wide	10 @ 6" wide	11 @ 5" wide
Binding	7 @ 2" wide	8 @ 2" wide	9 @ 2" wide	10 @ 2" wide	11 @ 2" wide

Note: The border widths are the cut measurements.

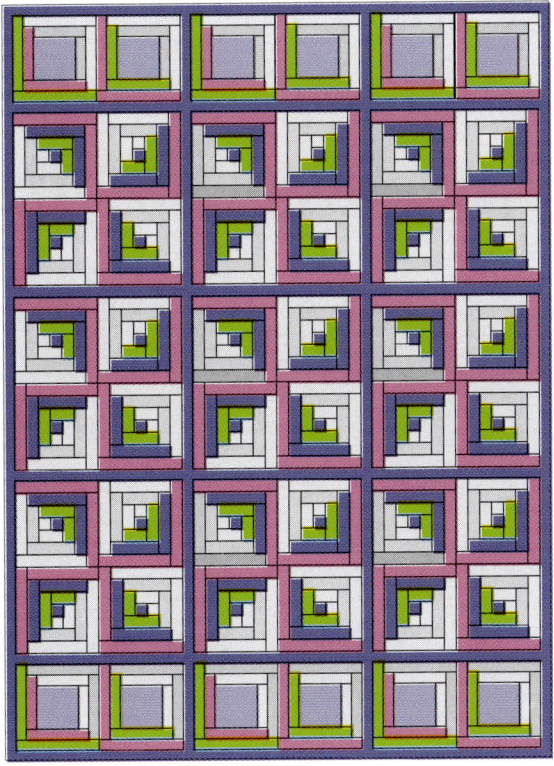

Lap Size Quilt Layout

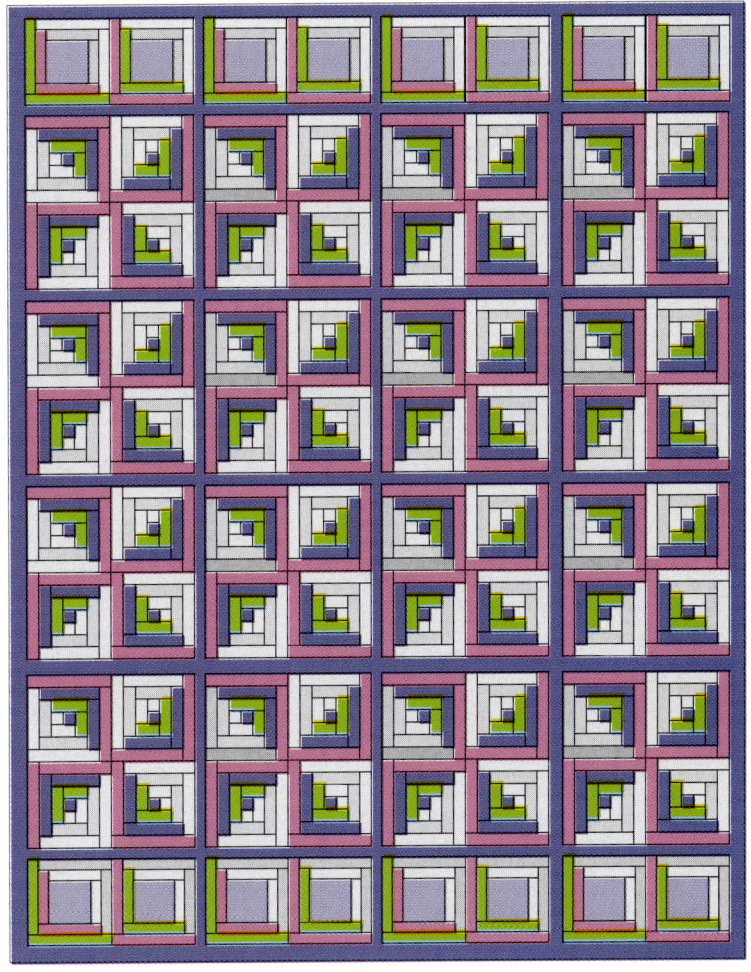

Twin/Full Layout

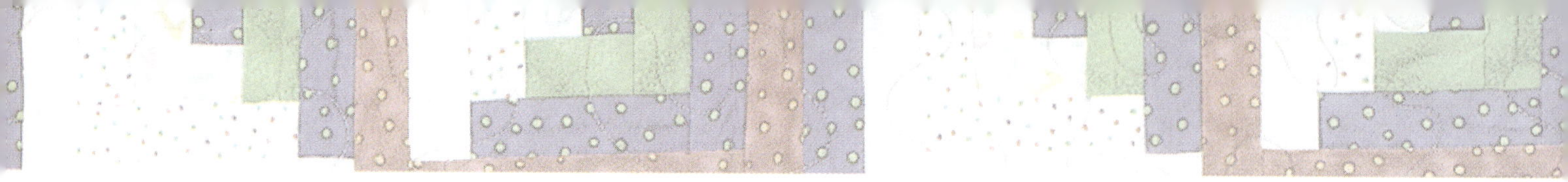

The following chart shows the yardage needed for each size quilt.

Yardage	Lap	Twin	Full	Queen	King
Animal fabric	½ yd	¾ yd	1 yd	1¼ yds	1½ yds
Lt letter print	½ yd	⅞ yd	⅞ yd	1 yd	1¼ yds
Lt dot print	¾ yd	1 yd	1 yd	1½ yds	1¾ yds
Lt cloud print	1 yd	1½ yds	1½ yds	2 yds	2½ yds
Dk blue	⅞ yd	1 yd	1 yd	1½ yds	1⅞ yds
Dk green	⅞ yd	1¼ yds	1¼ yds	1⅝ yds	2 yds
Dk pink	1¼ yd	1⅞ yds	1⅞ yds	2½ yds	3⅛ yds
Dk blue sashing	⅞ yd	1⅜ yds	2 yds	1¾ yds	1⅝ yds
Lt green border	1¼ yd	1¾ yds	2¼ yds	1¾ yds	1⅝ yds
Binding fabric	½ yd	⅝ yd	⅝ yd	¾ yd	⅞ yds
Batting	twin-size	twin-size	full-size	queen-size	king-size

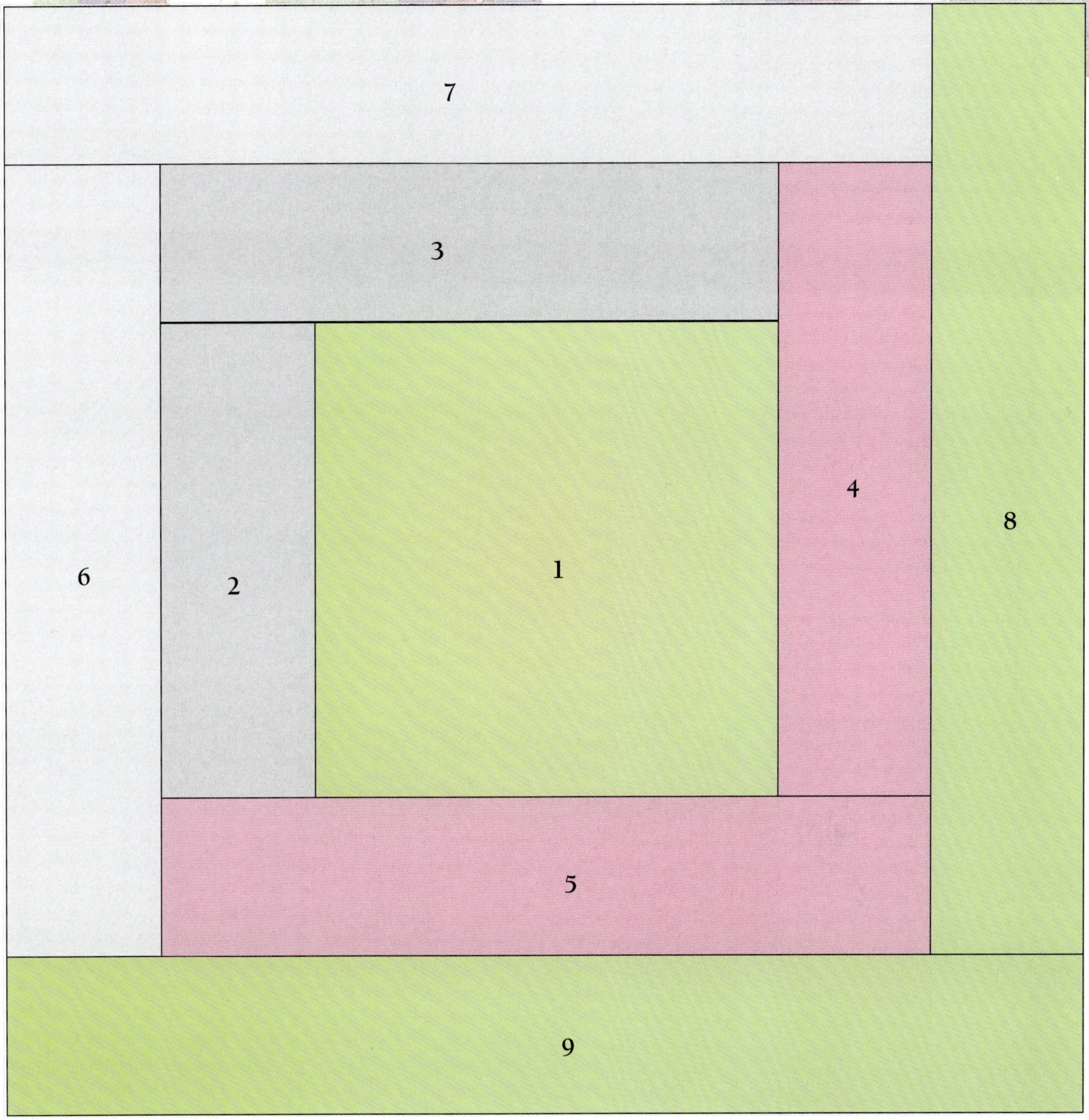

Baby Pinwheels Block 1

Block Diagram

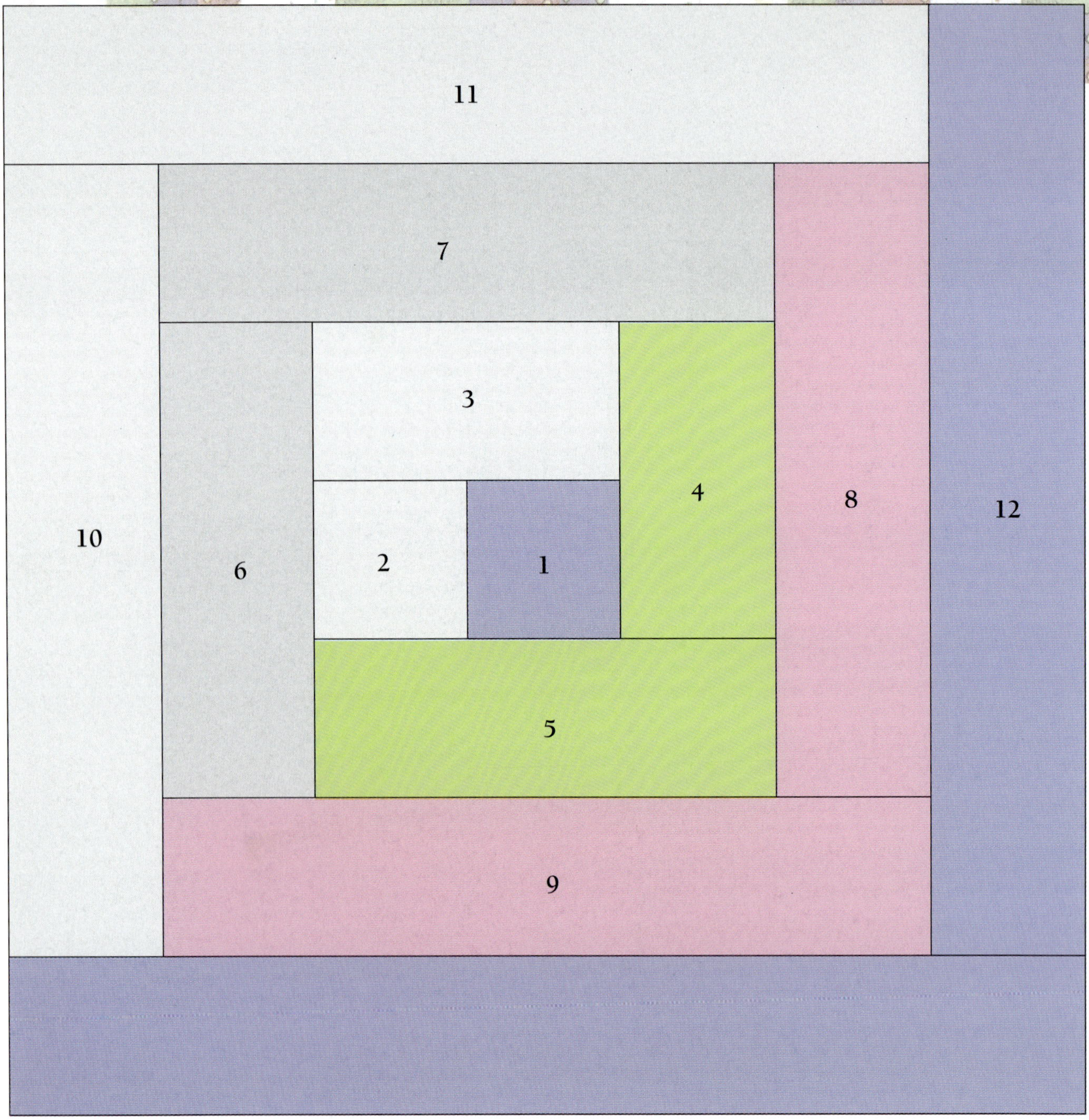

Baby Pinwheels Block 2

Block Diagram

48

O Christmas Tree

Approximate Size: 54" x 68"
Lap size setting (shown): 6 x 8
Number of Blocks: 48

Materials

⅜ yd gold print
1 yd red print
1½ yds assorted dk green prints
1¼ yds assorted med green prints
1 yd med blue print
1½ yds assorted lt blue prints
⅜ yd border 1 fabric
1¼ yds border 2 fabric or 2½ yds of assorted dk green fabrics for pieced border
½ yd binding fabric
3¼ yds backing fabric
twin-size batting
9" square of paper-backed fusible web

Cutting Requirements

Note: All strips include ½" seam allowance.
Cut the following 2"-wide strips for piecing:
One strip, gold print
Three strips, red print
22 strips, assorted dk green prints
20 strips, assorted med green prints
21 strips, assorted lt to med blue prints
15 strips, med blue print

Fussy cut the following 4" squares:
12 squares, novelty print

Cut the following border and binding strips:
Five 2"-wide strips, border 1 fabric
*Six 6"-wide strips, border 2 fabric
Seven 2½"-wide strips, binding fabric

*The photographed quilt shows a border made up of 1"-wide finished strips sewn together. To make this border, cut 40 2"-wide strips. Directions are given on page 51.

Quilt Diagram

49

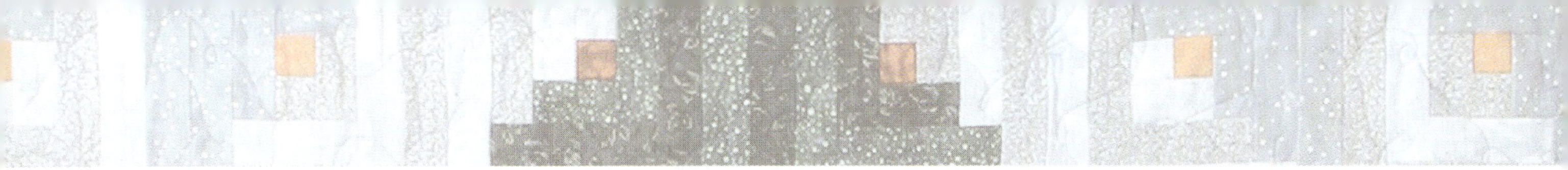

Instructions

Note: Read Working with Flannel: An Overview, page 4 before beginning.

1. Refer to How to Make a Foundation-Pieced Block, pages 6 to 7, and make twelve Log Cabin Blocks using pattern on page 53.
2. Make 36 Log Cabin blocks using pattern on page 54 referring to Block Diagrams on page 54 and 55 for color refernces.
3. Arrange blocks in eight rows of six blocks according to photograph.
4. Sew blocks together in rows, then sew rows together. Press seams in alternate directions.
5. Measure quilt top lengthwise. Piece 2"-wide border strips to achieve needed length (refer to Making a Quilt Top, page 8, for piecing border strips); repeat for another strip. Sew strips to opposite sides of quilt top. Press seams toward border.
6. Measure quilt top crosswise, including borders just added. Piece 2"-wide border strips to achieve needed length; repeat for another strip. Sew strips to top and bottom of quilt top. Press seams toward border.
7. Repeat steps 5 and 6 with 6"-wide strips for second border.

Tip: To make pieced border, sew assorted 2"-wide green strips together in sets of six, **Fig 1**; make 38 sets. Press seams open to reduce bulk. Cut across strip sets at 6" intervals, **Fig 2**. Measure quilt top lengthwise; sew sets together to achieve length needed for two border strips, **Fig 3**. Sew to opposite sides of quilt top. Measure quilt top crosswise, including the borders just added. Sew strips sets together to achieve length needed for two border strips. Sew to top and bottom of quilt top.

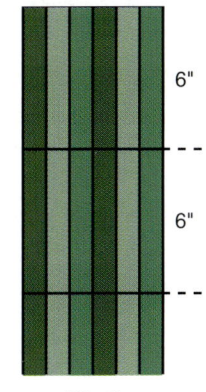

Fig 2

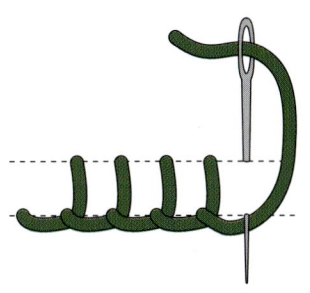

Fig 3

8. Trace Star pattern (page 55) onto paper side of fusible web. Following manufacturer's directions, iron to wrong side of gold print fabric. Peel off paper backing, position at top of tree and iron to quilt top. Use a Blanket stitch by hand, **Fig 4**, or machine to outline edge of star.
9. Finish quilt referring to Finishing Your Quilt, pages 9 to 11.

Alternate Size

The following yardages and measurements are for a twin-size quilt.

Approximate Size: 68" x 96"
Setting: 8 x 12
Number of Blocks: 96

Materials

⅜ yd gold print
⅜ yd red print
2⅝ yds assorted dk green prints
1¾ yds assorted med green prints
1⅝ yds med blue print
2 yds assorted lt blue prints
½ yd border 1 fabric
1⅝ yds border 2 fabric or 3⅛ yds of assorted dk green fabrics for pieced border
½ yd binding fabric
3¼ yds backing fabric
twin-size batting

Cutting Requirements

Note: All strips include ½" seam allowance.
Cut the following 2"-wide strips for piecing:

Two strips, gold print
Four strips, red print
46 strips, assorted dk green prints
30 strips, assorted med green prints
33 strips, assorted lt to med blue prints
27 strips, med blue print

Fussy cut the following 4" squares:

36 squares, novelty print

Cut the following border and binding strips:

Eight 2"-wide strips, border 1 fabric
*Nine 6"-wide strips, border 2 fabric
Nine 2½"-wide strips, binding fabric

*To make the pieced border made up of 1"-wide finished strips sewn together, cut 54 2"-wide strips. Directions are given above.

Fig 1
Assorted green fabrics

Fig 4
Blanket Stitch

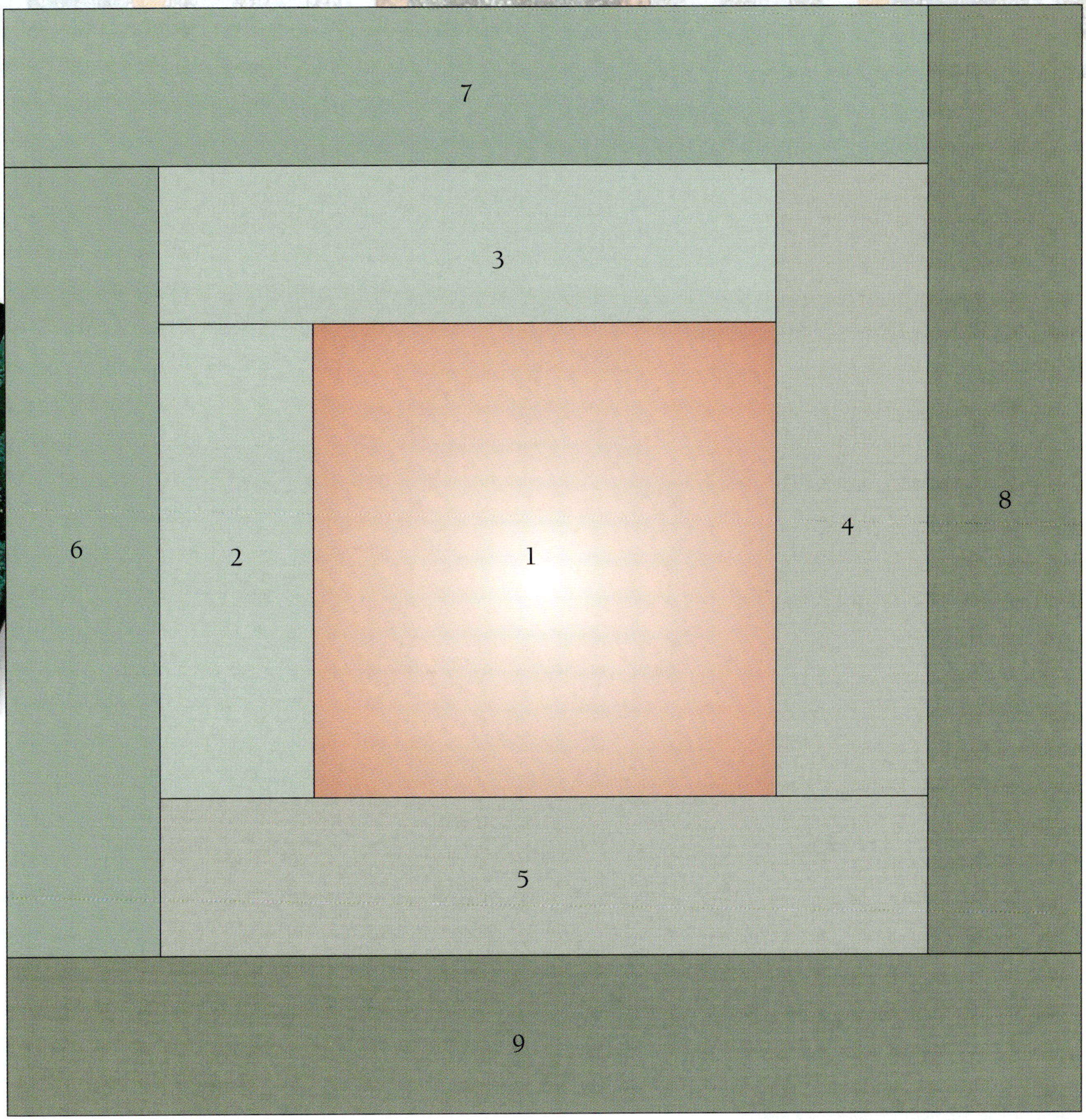

O Christmas Tree Block 1

Block Diagram

Make 12

53

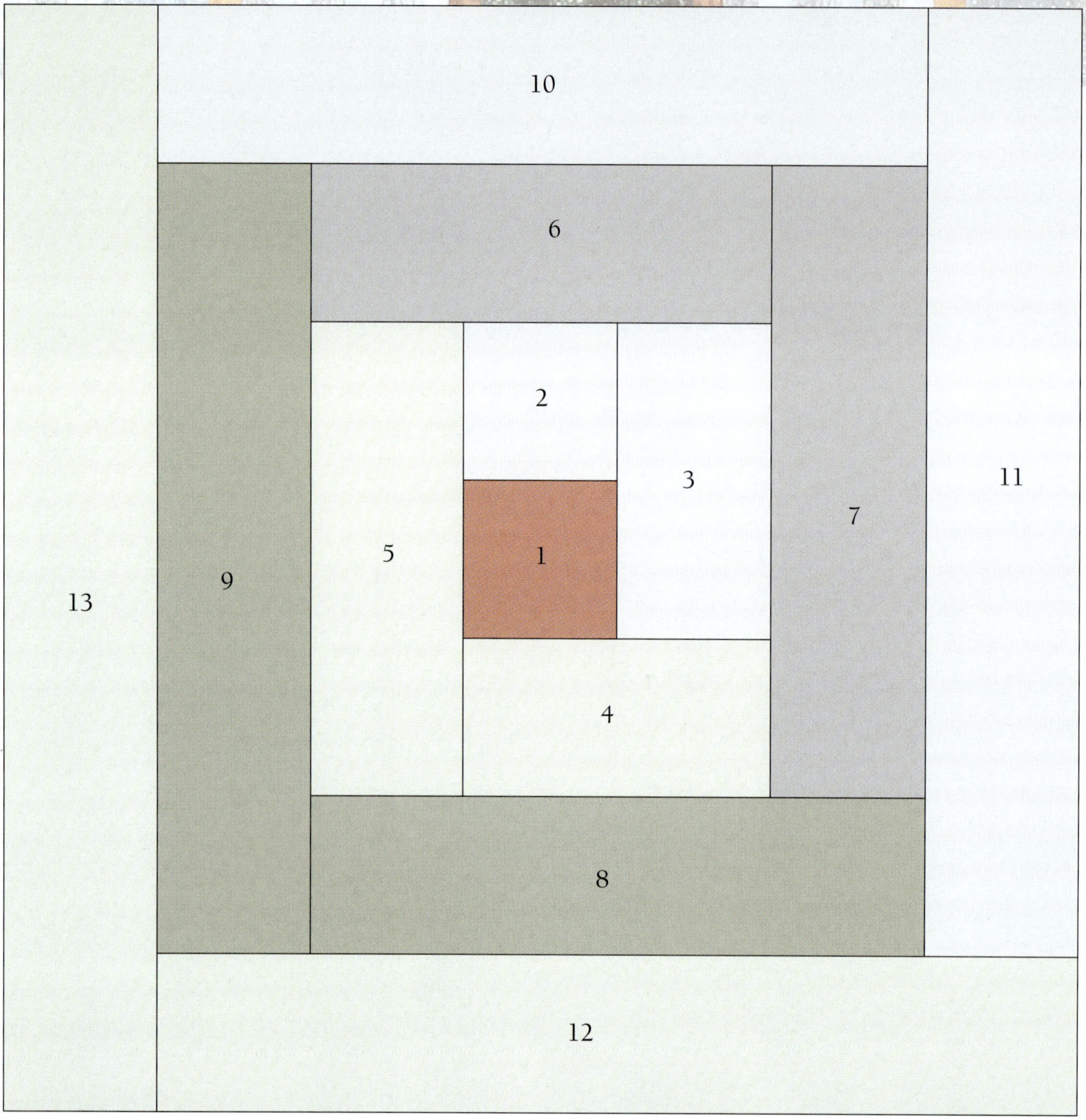

O Christmas Tree Block 2

Make 18   Make 8   Make 8

Block Diagrams

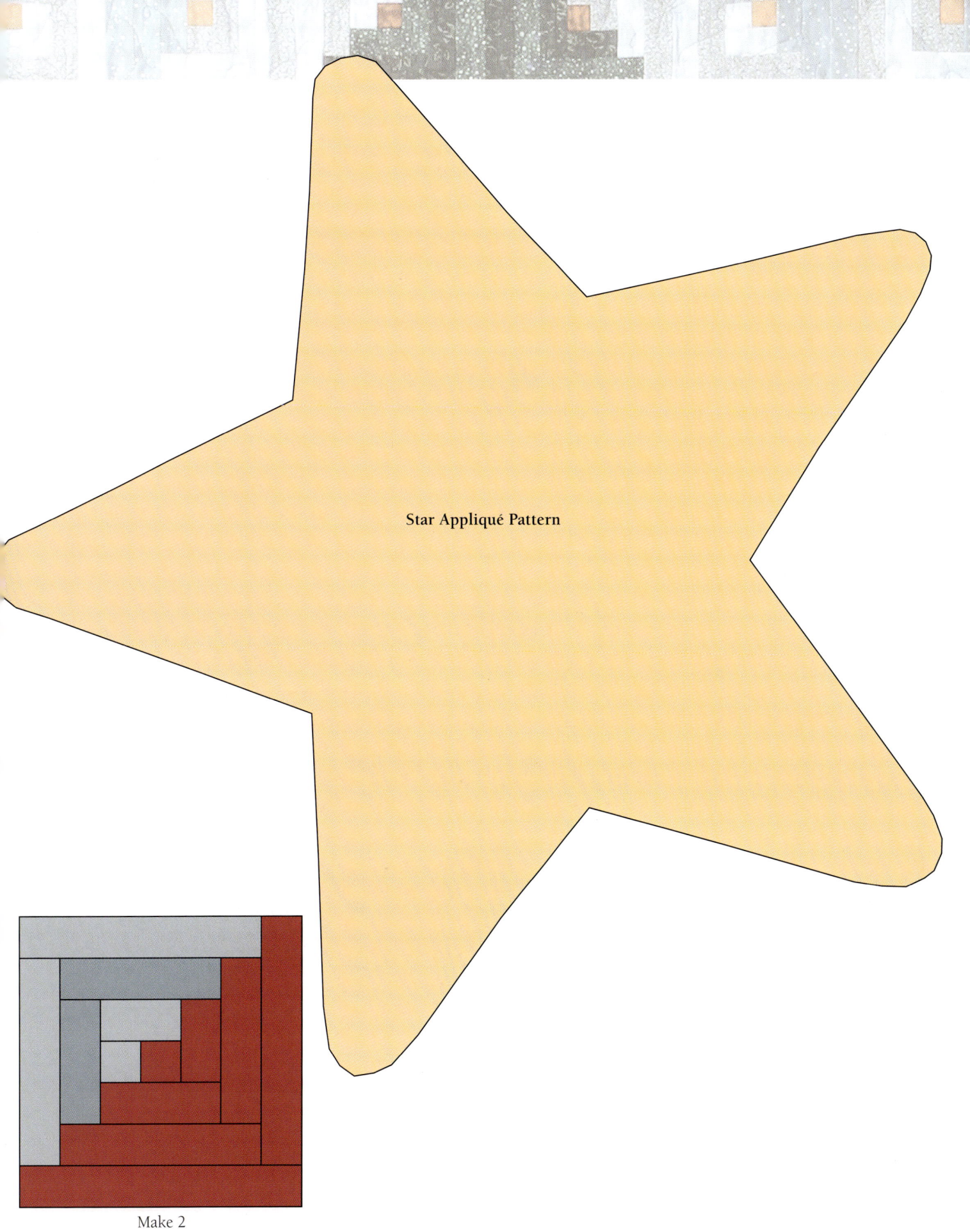

Star Appliqué Pattern

Make 2

Springtime Floral

Approximate Size: 50½" x 60½"
Lap Size Diagonal Setting: 4 x 5
Number of Blocks: 20

Materials

Note: The fabric amounts given are based on what is needed for this project. Due to flannel shrinkage, you may want to purchase at least ¼ to ½ yd more of each fabric.

¼ yd yellow
¼ yd lt pink
½ yd dk pink
⅝ yd purple
½ yd lt green
⅝ yd dk green
2½ yds lt background
⅜ yd border 1
⅞ yd border 2
⅜ yd binding
3 yds backing
Twin-size batting

Cutting Requirements

Note: All strips include ½" seam allowance.

Cut the following strips for piecing:

Note: The strip widths may be wider than necessary for some blocks. Trim fabric as you sew referring to the Foundation piecing instructions, pages 6 to 8.

Two 2½"-wide strips, yellow
Three 2½"-wide strips, lt pink
Five 3½"-wide strips, dk pink
Five 4½"-wide strips, purple
Five 3"-wide strips, lt green
Six 3"-wide strips, dk green
16 2"-wide strips, lt background

Continued on page 58

Quilt Diagram

Cut the following strips for setting triangles:
Seven 6½"-wide strips, lt background
(Cut into 40 squares, then cut in half diagonally for triangles.)

Cut the following border and binding strips:
Five 2½"-wide strips, border 1 fabric
Six 5"-wide strips, border 2 fabric
Six 2"-wide strips, binding

Instructions

Note: *Read Working with Flannel: An Overview, page 4 before beginning. Use a ½" seam allowance for sewing.*

1. Refer to How to Make a Foundation-Pieced Block, pages 6 to 8, and make five of each flower Log Cabin block using patterns on pages 61 to 64.
2. Sew a background triangle to opposite sides of a flower block; press open. Sew background triangles to remaining sides; press, **Fig 1**.
3. Trim blocks so the points of the flower blocks are ½" from edge, **Fig 2**.
4. Repeat steps 2 and 3 for remaining blocks.
5. Arrange blocks in five rows of four blocks according to photograph (or your own desired layout).
6. Sew blocks together in rows; then sew rows together. Press seams in alternate directions.
7. Measure quilt top lengthwise; piece 2½"-wide border strips to achieve needed length (refer to Making a Quilt Top, page 8, for piecing border strips); repeat for another strip. Sew strips to opposite sides of quilt top. Press seams toward border.
8. Measure quilt top crosswise, including borders just added; piece 2½"-wide border strips to achieve needed length; repeat for another strip. Sew strips to top and bottom of quilt top. Press seams toward border.
9. Repeat for second border with 5"-wide strips.
10. Finish quilt referring to Finishing Your Quilt, pages 9 to 11.

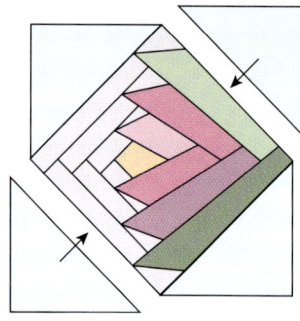

Fig 1

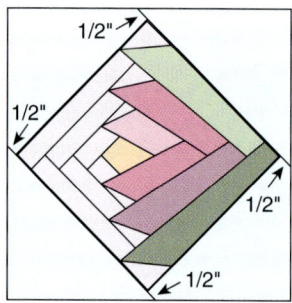

Fig 2

Other Sizes

The following chart shows number of strips needed to make the number of Log Cabin blocks for five other quilt sizes. The border widths are the cut measurements.

	Wall hanging/Baby	Twin	Full	Queen	King
Size	45½" x 45½"	70¼" x 90"	80" x 100"	93" x 103"	106" x 106"
Setting	4 x 4	6 x 8	7 x 9	8 x 9	9 x 9
Blocks	16	48	63	72	81
Yellow	1 @ 2½"	3 @ 2½"	4 @ 2½"	4 @ 2½"	5 @ 2½"
Lt pink	3 @ 2½"	7 @ 2½"	9 @ 2½"	10 @ 2½"	11 @ 2½"
Dk pink	5 @ 3½"	11 @ 3½"	15 @ 3½"	17 @ 3½"	19 @ 3½"
Purple	4 @ 3¼"	12 @ 3¼"	14 @ 3¼"	16 @ 3¼"	18 @ 3¼"
Lt green	4 @ 3"	11 @ 3"	13 @ 3"	15 @ 3"	17 @ 3"
Dk green	5 @ 3"	13 @ 3"	16 @ 3"	19 @ 3"	21 @ 3"
Background	14 @ 2"	38 @ 2"	50 @ 2"	57 @ 2"	65 @ 2"
*Background (triangles)	6 @ 6½"	18 @ 6½"	21 @ 6½"	24 @ 6½"	27 @ 6½"
Border 1	4 @ 2"	8 @ 2½"	9 @ 2½"	9 @ 3"	10 @ 3½"
Border 2	4 @ 3"	9 @ 5"	10 @ 5"	10 @ 6"	11 @ 7"
Binding	4 @ 2"	9 @ 2"	10 @ 2"	10 @ 2"	11 @ 2"

*Cut 6½" squares, then cut diagonally into triangles.

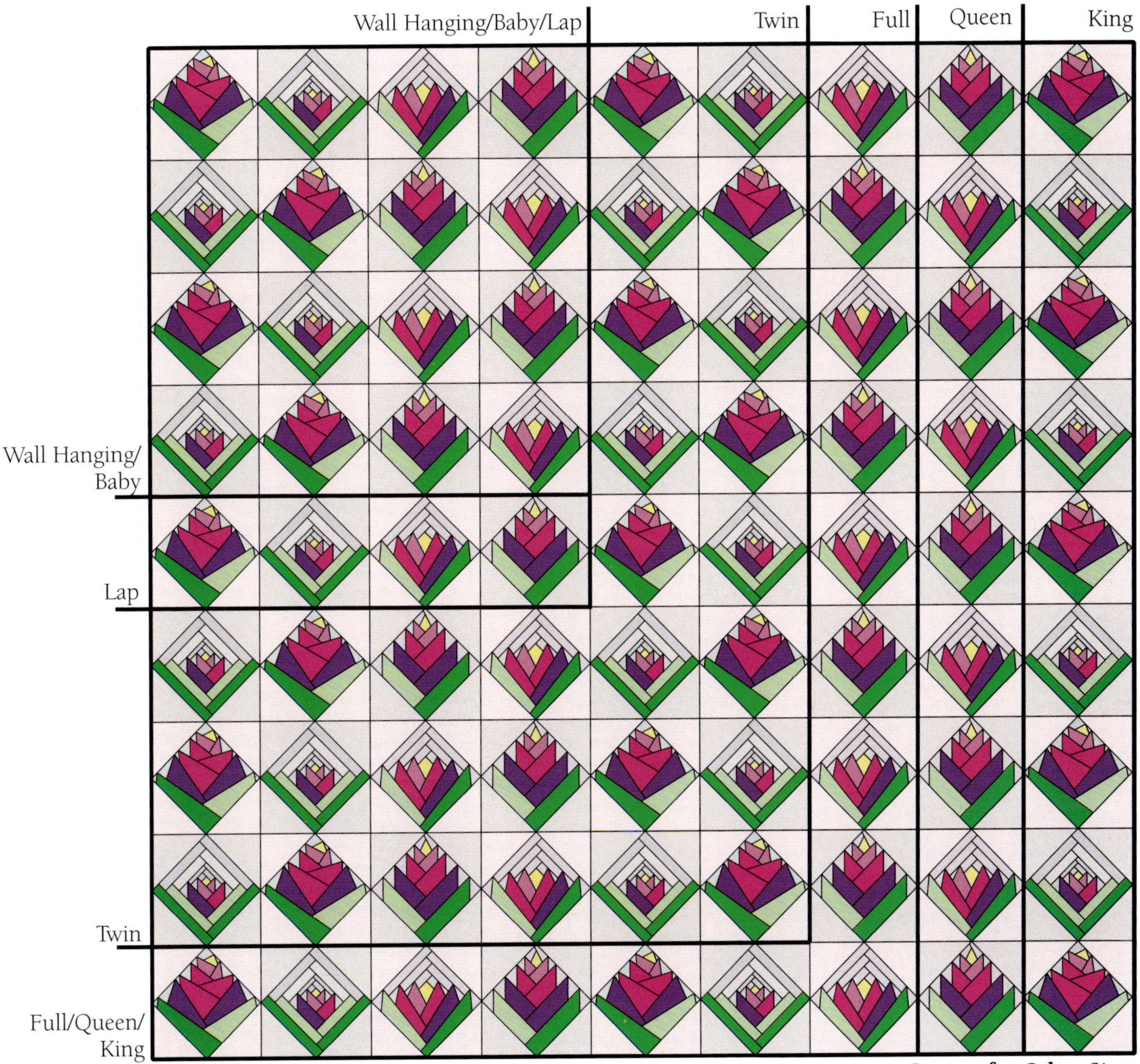

The following chart shows the yardage needed for each size quilt.

Yardage	Wall hanging/Baby	Twin	Full	Queen	King
Yellow	⅛ yd	¼ yd	⅜ yd	⅜ yd	⅜ yd
Lt pink	¼ yd	½ yd	¾ yd	¾ yd	⅞ yd
Dk pink	½ yd	1⅛ yds	1½ yds	1¾ yds	1⅞ yds
Purple	½ yd	1⅛ yds	1⅜ yds	1½ yds	1¾ yds
Lt green	½ yd	1 yd	1⅛ yds	1⅜ yds	1½ yds
Dk green	½ yd	1⅛ yds	1½ yds	1⅝ yds	1⅞ yds
Background	2⅛ yds	5⅜ yds	6⅞ yds	7¾ yds	8¾ yds
Border 1	¼ yd	⅝ yd	¾ yd	⅞ yd	1 yd
Border 2	⅜ yd	1¼ yds	1½ yds	1¾ yds	2¼ yds
Binding	¼ yd	½ yd	⅝ yd	⅝ yd	¾ yd
Backing	2 yds	5¼ yds	7 yds	8¼ yds	9 yds

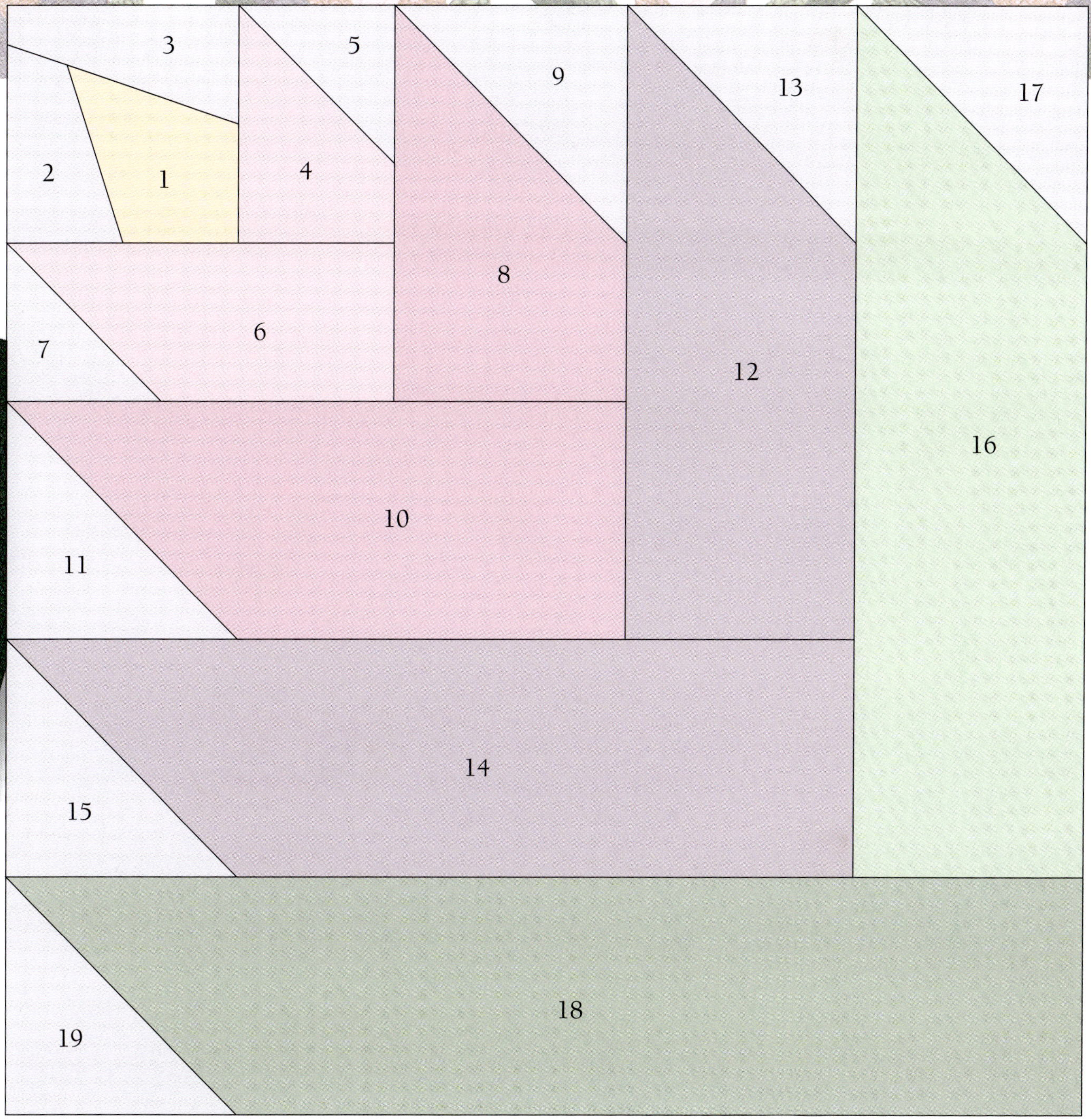

Springtime Floral Block 1

Block Diagram

61

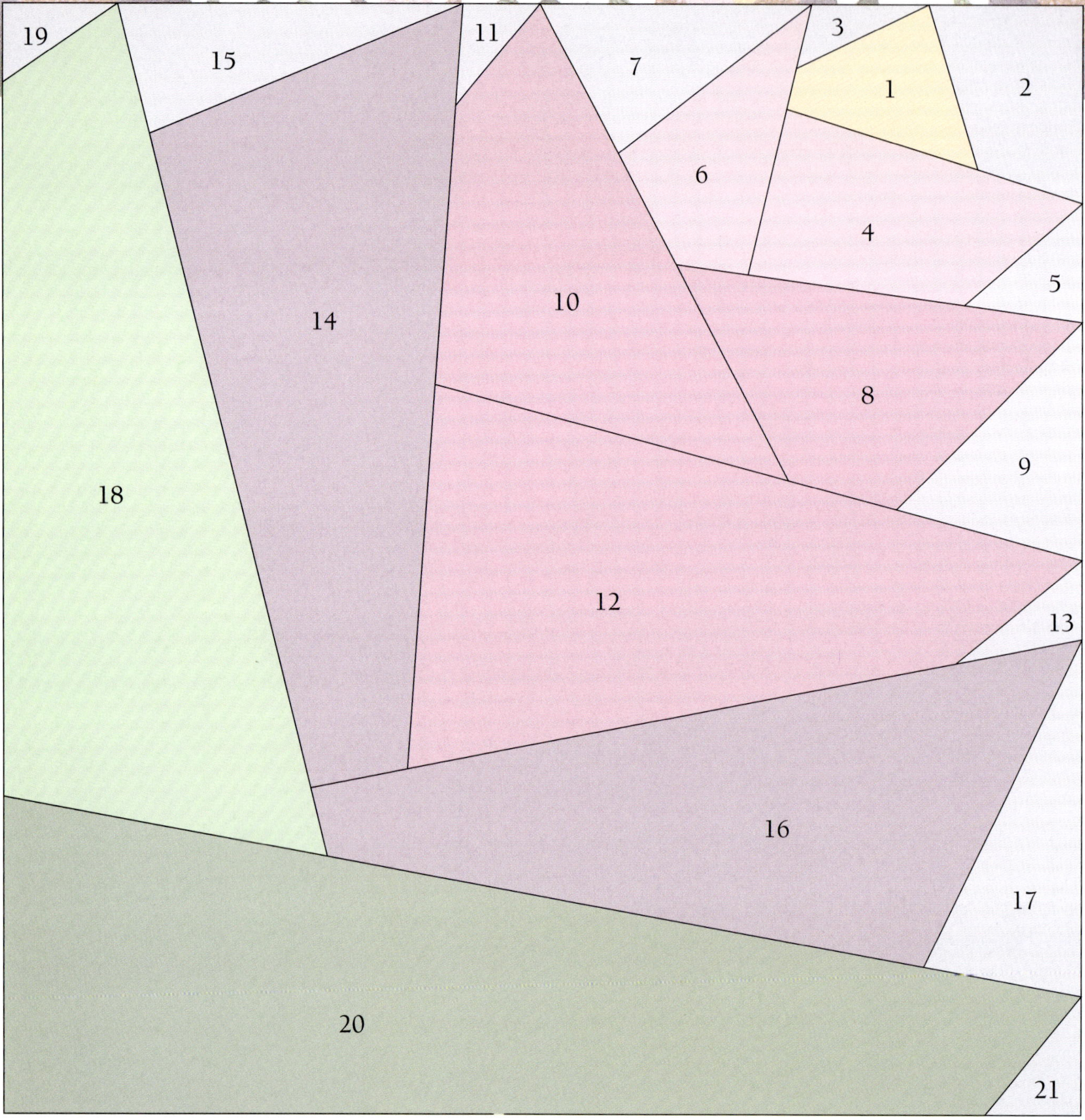

Springtime Floral Block 2

Block Diagram

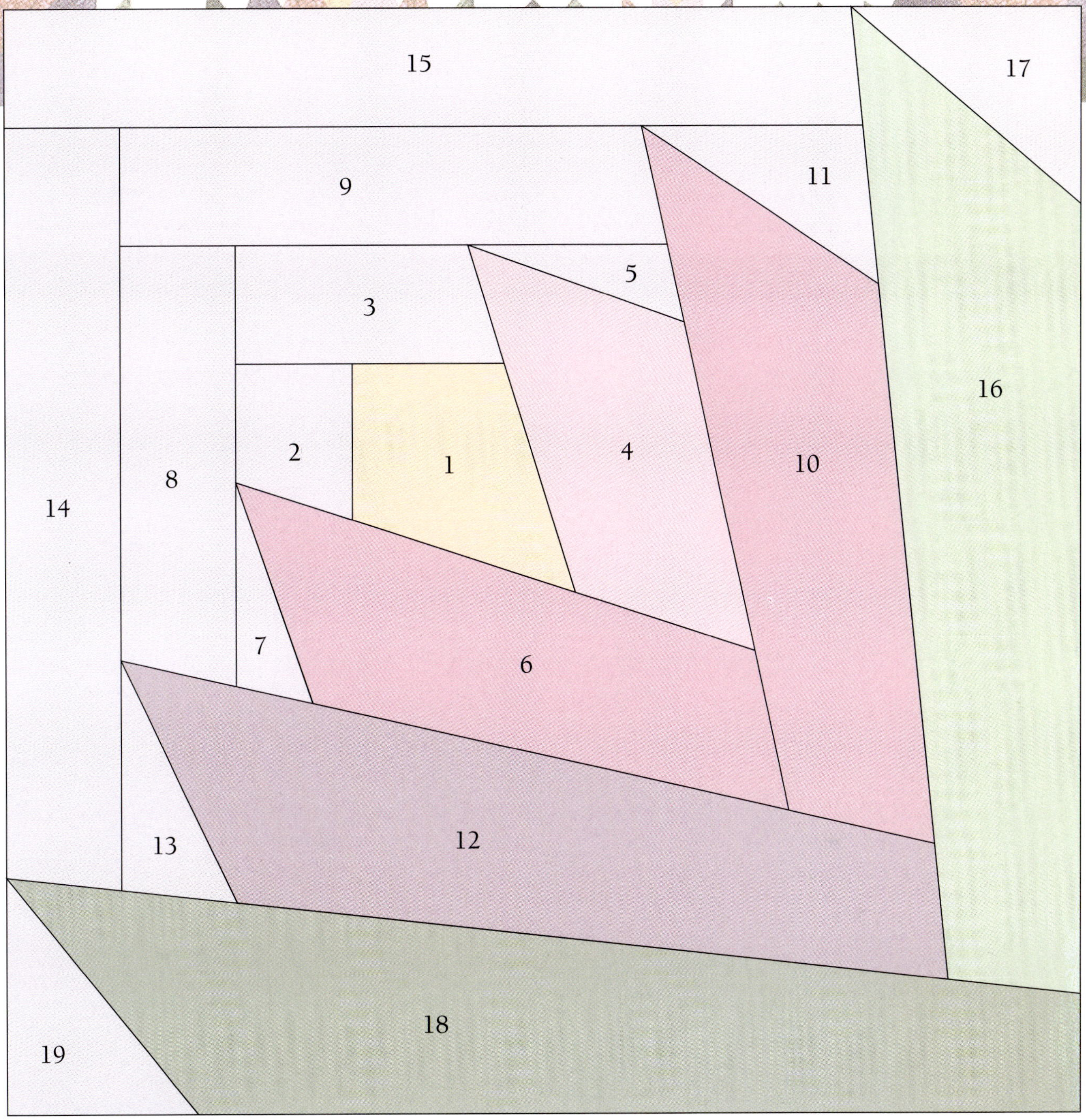

Springtime Floral Block 3

Block Diagram

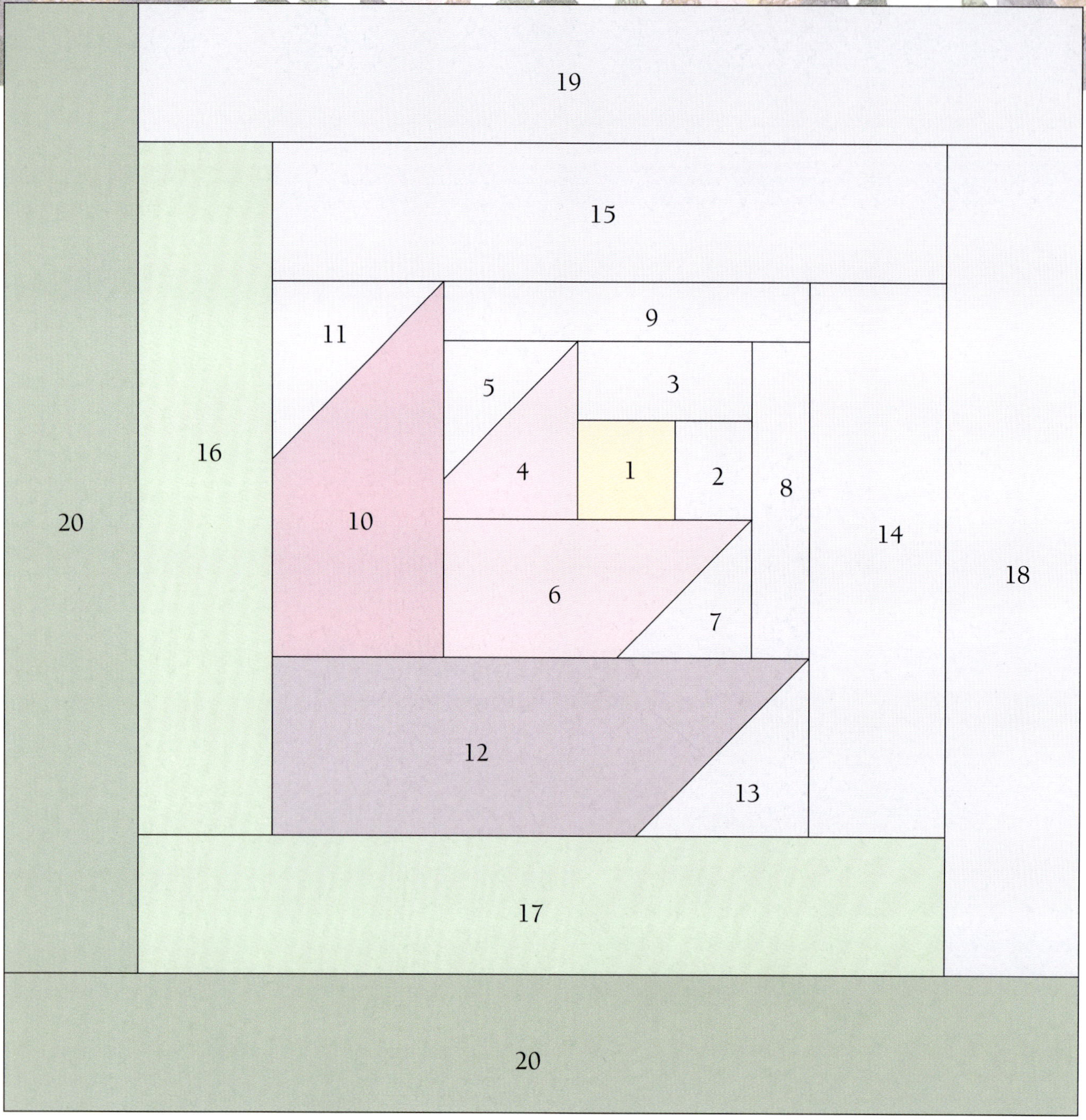

Springtime Floral Block 4

Block Diagram